Boots and Saddle

by

Ron Bradshaw

First published in 1992
by
Richard Netherwood Limited.
Fulstone Barn, New Mill, Huddersfield HD7 7DL.
Copyright © R.W.Bradshaw 1992
Printed and bound in Gorenjski tisk, Kranj, Slovenia

To my ever loving wife Dorothea
for her undying devotion,
Her fortitude and forbearance,
and my own faith in her unfailing forgiveness.

To all the many walking and cycling friends whose names have
escaped me over the passage of time, and to those others who
contributed so much towards the ultimate successes of the
Rossendale Road Club.

Quotations from:
The *Scout* magazine 1935.

The Chief, The Life Story of Baden Powel by Eileen K. Wade.
Walfe Publishing 1975.

Speaking from Memory Bernard Newman. Herbert Jenkins 1960.

FOREWORD

by

Mike Harding

The Northern working class has had a long love affair with the countryside that probably stems from the fact that our ancestors were all originally country dwellers driven into towns by the enclosures of common land and by the great magnet of the new industrial workshops of the world that were growing like cankers along the river valleys.

Manchester, Bolton, Rochdale and Oldham were nothing but muddy villages until King Cotton came along with his smoking chimneys and thumping machines, and the men and women imprisoned by what William Blake called 'cogs tyrannic' hungered for the hills and the open road. And they took to the moors and roads in ever greater numbers so that by the 1930's in Britain, journalists could talk about 'Ramblingitis' the stations were crammed every Sunday morning with hikers off to the hills and the roads were full of wheelmen (and women) cranking their way out of the filth of the industrial towns out into the moors and valleys of the north.

Like every movement the outdoor movement had its scribes, its poets and balladeers, Tom Stephenson wrote literally millions of words on the outdoors, a textile worker from Lancashire, he became the most prolific writer and campaigner and it is to him of course that we owe the Pennine Way. Benny Rothman has written a fine account of the outdoor movement in the 30's in his Kinder Mass Trespass while the press-officer on that trespass was Ewan McColl, who with Joan Littlewood created a new British theatre and wrote that fanfare for the common man and that marching song of walkers, climbers and cyclists everywhere The Manchester Rambler.

Dead in line with that very Northern tradition Ron Bradshaw has written the best account I have read of a life lived for the romance of the road and the hills. It will bring back the smell of heather and the feel of a road spinning away under your feet to all of us who read it on dark winter evenings and grey days. It is a full and rich story of days of boots and saddle written from heart, feet and pant's seat and none the worse for that.

CONTENTS

First recorded in my log book July 1943:

Oh, I ha' strayed thro' many a land
And gazed on some scenes divine!
There's naught so wonderful or so grand
As yon wonderful North o' mine.

And steer me the ship to the North, I say
And show me the northern shore
And let me hear a northern bell
Ring clear on its cliff once more.

And let me see the Northern fells
And hear the Northern streams
And sit where a forest fairy tells
The weird old woodland dreams.

To the wondering, waking babies of spring
By the side of a haunted burn
What time the linnet begins to sing
And the first green comes to the fern.

Steer me the ship, good pilot, steer
Where the Northern sea birds fly
Steer where the great grey skies stretch clear!
For I am, a Northman, I!

(Author unknown.)

CHAPTER 1.

LANCASHIRE ROOTS

Comfortably ensconced in a plush armchair, deep in its snug luxury whilst meditating and gazing dreamily into a flickering fire is hardly the place to formulate, or less still pen narrations exemplifying the magnetic attractions of a life in the great outdoors. Through half closed eyes, drowsed by the ambience of a thermostatically controlled heat I chase visions across a vast canvas of mountain, lake, road and river. Smiling as the scenes rapidly change. The heaving of a bike over a six foot snow drift clad merely in a shirt and sweater to repel an icy north east wind across one's chest, and lightweight cycling shoes, ankle socks and a pair of corduroy shorts making a pathetic attempt to fight the Siberian elements of a North Pennine blizzard. Shorts that fitted ill over my spindly thighs had a nasty habit of encouraging every breath of these evil draughts to penetrate each nook, crevice and projectile that cowered in my nether regions. Underpants had not been invented at that time; or if they had, I couldn't afford them.

Uproariously funny we concluded at the time, in particular when sat around some youth hostel fire exchanging yarns in the evening. Likewise a situation when soaked to the skin, shivering like a half demented jackass you crash to the ground after misjudging the angle of wet tramlines in the middle of Glasgow.

Yes, these, and a thousand other recollections build up a vivid tapestry of life in the open air. And now, all but seventy years have slipped by, I sit back to recall at least, the highlights of a happy and eventful life, in the pursuit of what Chris Bonington has aptly described as, "an exercise to see what is on the other side of the hill."

I pick up a leaflet illuminating the merits of my native Rossendale Valley and its surroundings; Another, one of the touristic values of Bury my second home, and vividly recall the grime, the smog, the stinking rivers Irwell and Roch and marvel how, in so short a time span can such a transitional wonder come about. This very environment, today devoid of its myriad mill chimneys belching lung choking smoke was the very surroundings that we, in our formative years were encouraged at every opportunity to escape from. An exodus not only confined to the annual

wakes week, but to the fast growing army of youth that were taking to
the hills and the roads, either on foot or on cycle.

A second scan of these glossy brochures, recklessly distributed in an
effort to promote each and every councils claim to having replaced
industrial growth with that of imported tourism and local recreation, and
I ponder in reflective doubt. Nevertheless, it is there. Today's tourist
seeks not only sun and beach, or mountain and lake. Many are searching
for the remains of our industrial might; the towns where King Cotton and
King Coal reigned supreme and Britain's industrial wealth evolved. The
world moves so tremendously fast today, that history is considered
anything that happened a little over two generations past.

One small statistic in the reinstated Irwell Valleys railway time table
causes me to chuckle. The return fare for travel on this tourist attraction
from Bury to Rawtenstall is in the region of £5.00, a round distance of
eight miles. When the track was a double line through to Bacup, and I
held the hand of my parents in order to avoid being crushed in the
stampede for seats, the return excursion fares to Blackpool, a round trip
of some eighty miles were; day excursions, five shillings; half day
excursion, three shillings and sixpence; and evening excursion a matter
of two and sixpence only; In today's money, 25 pence, 18 pence and
13 pence!

It would have been within the normal bounds of intelligence to expect
inflation to play havoc with the pound sterling, but hard indeed, to
visualise the demise and eventual shutdown of the then ex East Lancashire branch line into the 'Golden Valley'.

And 'Golden' it had been in the nineteenth century, though not for the
colour of its corn or its botanical displays, but for the hard earned cash
that a hundred and more mills put into the hands of industrialists whose
factories spawned the Irwell and its fast flowing tributaries. Money they
took from these desecrated hillsides and rivers, to build mansions in
Southport, Lytham-St-Annes and the Lake District.

Yes, my brochure is staggeringly colourful. The sky is blue and the grass
is green; almost the green of a Sussex cricket pitch. The transition in half
a century is as unique as that evidenced in the first half of the last century,
and now the process has turned full circle.

But to witness a blue sky above any town between Bacup and
Rawtenstall, or to discover a blade of verdant grass in the 1920's, my
own formative years, it would likely mean packing up the sandwiches,

placing these in the inevitable brown paper carrier bag with string handles
and probably sporting the attributes of Harry Croppers the butcher, or
Duckworths the grocers, and setting out with what appeared to be half
the population of Waterfoot and heading for Waughs Well. On attaining
the higher reaches of Lench and the farms of Mrs. Clay and the
Davenports, the first sign of a blue sky would emerge, and then facing
down into the valley below, an insufferable pall of smog, whilst mill
chimneys poked their ugly tops through this morass of acrid filth.

At the well, high on the edge of Scout Moor stubbly grass poked up into
ones baggy short breeches, or ill fitting blue cotton knickers as the case
may be. Shortly the whole hillside was speckled with flat caps and 'plant
pot' hats. The whole outing became one big thrill. Tea was served from
the nearby farm in huge blue enamel jugs as sandwiches were eagerly
snatched from their white paper bags. Across the moors were dotted the
crumbling remains of abandoned farmhouses, their occupants having
relinquished them long ago, earning a more lucrative wage in the stone
quarries that mushroomed as industrialists demanded more and more
stone for the factories, then yet more again for the primitive dwellings that
would house the workers.

To define the fascination is difficult. Those days, as they were to any child
whose parents had the fortune of employment and their stomachs were
full, were sheer heaven. His environment means little to him at that stage
of his life. There were the days sitting in orderly fashion on row upon row
of wooden bench seats, up to equally white scrubbed top tables, to
savage mountains of currant buns in the Chapel 'Rooms'. Or to stare up
in amazement at our parents who let their hair down and at some I.L.P.
social, sang their heads off in the 'Labour' rooms above Holts piano
shop.

And what of the shining monster that stood outside his shop? A motor
car no less, with huge gleaming headlamps polished to perfection and a
running board that I doubt I could reach even if I dare try. No, Mr. Holt
would not need to board the tram. He needn't soil his shoes either in the
horse dung that grew faster than any ant hill in the streets of our valley
at that time. The massive cart horses too with their fine array of brasses
were as regular an institution as the wailing factory hooters that vied with
each other for the piercest shrills at 7.30 in the morning, and again at 5.30
in the evening. Only the disconcerted efforts at midnight on New Year's
Eve would prove more devastatingly effective.

But if the grass was not green on the hillsides of our valley, then it was both further north in the charm of the Yorkshire Dales, and to the south in the rich pasture lands of Cheshire. This we now knew. We had been told it all by the great Ward Ogden, and this particularly imposing character was really someone to listen to.

Along with other militant seekers of the rights to access of our many public footpaths, he was a founder member of the P.P.P.S. (The Pennine Paths Preservation Society), and as young walkers with the local Ramblers Association we were all proud to sport the little metal badge. Ward Ogden would preach the gospel of re-opening rights of way, and carry with him permanently, a pair of World War One barbed wire cutters to mark his presence. I don't recall him ever being in the hands of the law, but several of his compatriots in Derbyshire were. Nevertheless, for their undying efforts we have them to thank in particular for the existence of the Pennine Way, a forerunner of the many long distance paths of today.

'Ward' I am sure set many a lad on the way to becoming an outdoor fanatic. Along with Fred Rees, a lifetime close friend, I was certainly one of them.

Recollections of my earliest thrust into the great outdoors are now somewhat hazy, though memory recalls a return from an enlightening stay with my Grandma in Bury. The visit had awoken my senses to the fact that no two towns were alike. This one apparently did have something other than the inevitable cobblestones and tramlines; it still had gas lit streets, whilst our town boasted electric lamp standards. Following a close scrutiny for several nights I discovered that the man with the hooked pole did not come round any more; but that the interior of the glass surround housed a pilot light and presumably the gas company turned on the main supply at the appropriate time in the evening. All very intriguing to a youngster brought up for some six years among the conveniences of the new electrical age.

The overall realisation was, that outside our valley there were endless adventures to seek, new towns, fresh hills and even a people that differed in their dialect. A tangible sign that curiosity was rapidly fostering a desire to travel. Shortly it would be insatiable. Unbridled interest in hills and rivers followed as the ability to travel by foot beyond the periphery of Rossendale's clutches, grew unchecked. Hikes to Pendle Hill, across 'Wuthering Heights', along Winter Hill and to the towers of Grant and

Peel; sentinels guarding approach to the Irwell Valley.

All these delights abounded, and I recall well my father's exaltation of the great Baden Powell, whose Boy Scouts movement aimed high in the pursuit of open air activities and clean living. At the early age of seven, I was sufficiently indoctrinated to crave the day I would reach the age, and be eligible to join the band of Wolf Cubs, whose happy youngsters served their apprenticeship to future scouting. Then by the time the great day arrived, the blood flowing through my veins was well and truly tainted, stained with the peat of the moor lands, and the iron from the hill streams that cascaded into the rivers of the West Pennines.

Lord Baden Powell was born in the year 1857. Following a very full life, and at the mature age of 51, he founded The Boy Scout Movement. Hitherto, and in the years to follow, his whole existence was to exemplify the true course of an officer and gentleman of the times.

By the time I was initiated into the movement in 1930, Baden Powell had attained the ripe old age of 73. I could but wonder at the time, in what way had this truly enigmatic gentleman come to cast such a profound impact on the likes of we dedicated youngsters of that epoch. Why the spellbinding devotion and a total commitment to the movement. From whence came the euphoria of burning wood smoke, the magic of flickering shadows across the green canvas tents at nightfall and the camaraderie of a camp fire gathering at dusk. Of the eerie call of an owl or the ghoulish croak of a bull frog and the incessant babblings of cascading waters in a mountain stream. A sing song of nature that never dies. And all this long before the transistor radio killed the desire to lie, and to listen.

That was the life of Baden Powell in the South African veldt. An ontology he accepted as being a direct challenge to the squalor he witnessed on his frequent returns to Britain. For ever he became to despair for the youths of his native country that grovelled in the back streets of Victorian inner cities. He felt sympathy for the 'Tommy', the innocent who would volunteer willingly to fight the Afrikaner for British supremacy in the Cape provinces. He knew well they would be a sitting target in blatantly conspicuous scarlet. Uniforms of such pretension would do little to strike fear into a Boer marksman sat high in a tree and totally inconspicuous in camouflaged clothing. And until the powers that be discarded a battle uniform that invited carnage, a heavy toll of British lives would fall to a sniper's bullet or a Zulu spear.

Thus Baden Powell and his contemporaries were to initiate a complete reversal in the attitudes to the military dress of our European soldiery. The military stratagem of fanfaronade was well and good on the parade ground; no longer was it practical on the battle field.

A further and alarming vacuum was the Tommies lack of initiative of self survival. To Colonel Powell, a past master in this art it was tantamount to suicide in the fight for existence in hostile territory. Like all mortals of the Germanic temperament these brave soldiers were supreme in their willing acceptance of orders to line up in ranks for slaughter, but when it came to a lone existence in the jungle with no sergeant of officer to bully them they were at a pathetic loss.

That the industrial squalor, and city environment had its roots in the degeneration of European manhood Baden Powell had no doubt, and one day he would set about mustering the youth of Edwardian Britain and lay foundation to a new and healthier society.

When in 1910, a mere two years after initiating his dream and witnessing it grow to the phenomenal number of 123,000 and that, worldwide, he took time to look back on his career.

He had been the hero of Mafeking during the Boer War; alone he had mapped a wild 600 mile frontier land in Natal; had seen service on the North West frontier of India, and in Afghanistan; hunted wild animal in India, and spied for the British army in Russia.

He described the dawn of his scouting movement as his second life, and wrote; "where is there a boy, even in these materialistic times, to whom the call of the wild and open road does not appeal?" "Maybe it is the primitive instinct, anyway, it is there. With that key a great door may be unlocked, if it is only to admit fresh air and sunshine into lives that were otherwise grey."

His book "Scouting for Boys", published along with the founding had previously taken the form of 'Aid to Scouting' in 1899, a publication he wrote for the use of soldier training. From then, and along with the weekly 'Scout' magazine, the book was to read by millions of eager boys the world over.

At the 'Coming of Age' jamboree, held in Arrow Park, Birkenhead he was to receive many gifts, amongst them a peerage; but the star attraction was the Rolls Royce car and trailer caravan. The car became known as the 'Penny Jam Roll', and the reason for that was that scouts the world over had donated one penny each, a subscription that was strictly limited.

The red haired and freckled youngster Baden Powell, known to his school chums as 'Bathing Towel' was to earn worldwide admiration. He had no attraction to politics whatsoever and following the fame he achieved in the South African War, he was invited by Lord Roberts to stand for Parliament. He could not resist sending his cryptic reply by telegram. "Delighted..... Which side"!

At the ripe old age of 81 he left Britain to return to Africa; to the wide open spaces he adored. In 1941 he died under the very shadow of Mount Kenya, with the knowledge that over ten million youths across the world carried his message.

Later, in a farewell note discovered after his death, a small sign was observed. It was a small dot within a circle. That is the trekkers international sign meaning "Gone Home".

If my father held any objection whatsoever to the scouting movement it was but one, and that was what he termed the "drum banging image". He knew well the recruitment potential of bugle and drum; boys will follow them anywhere. He recalled the stark similarities that had dragged thousands of young men from their homes in 1915 to be slaughtered like cattle on the fields of Northern France and Belgium. That in itself was his one and only dissent, and shared by many of his friends who had fought and returned.

To the cause of healthy and clean living, and a marked guidance to care and understanding, incorporating an emphasis on outdoor activities, he was wholeheartedly in the movement's favour.

It so came about then, that on achieving the great milestone of accept-ability, that was the age of eight, the '24th Rossendale' the St. Annes (or Piercy) troop took in its newest recruit. A year following I would spend my first holiday under canvas, at that time a pastime partaken purely by soldierly and the like. The camping craze as we know it today was a far distant phenomenon, thus it may be opportune to digress a little at this stage and cast a nostalgic eye at the Rossendale I was born into in those very early twenties.

Waterfoot was my small town, and I first opened an inquisitive eye in the year 1922 to gaze round onto flagstone floors and a gas lit parlour. I'm sure my chubby little nose twitched at the ever prevailing stench of horse dung, both fresh and mature as it wafted from the adjoining railway cart horse stables. This little snippet of useless historical knowledge took place in the row of houses known as Foundry Vale, though I recall none of it as by the age of two, we had moved to the more salubrious surroundings of Edgside, and on to the council estate that provided houses with electric light and even a bathroom. It was said that new tenants from the demolished Bridleway slums kept coal in their baths. However, I never was able to substantiate the rumour! A little way down the avenue, doubtless as I struggled to learn the knack of thrashing a 'top and whip' a little girl was being born to my parents friends, the Rees's. Her name was to be Dorothea and her unfortunate destiny would be to marry the author of this narrative.

To achieve a concept however of life an a Lancashire valley such as our little town on the banks of the Irwell, it is first necessary to clear a little opening in the pall of acrid smoke that polluted the region from dawn until dusk. Then to fill one's nostrils with the over-riding permeation of cotton in its complex process of devilling, spinning, weaving, bleaching, dyeing and finishing at the multitude of mills that straddled the river banks. Our cobblestoned roads would witness the passage of far more cart horses than trams, let alone the motor car that was making a rare appearance. The possession of a bicycle was a sure sign of affluence. Locate yourself on the corner of Burnley Road and Bacup Road, in front of Harry Cropper's, the butcher and alongside the District Bank. Do this at 5.35p.m. on any weekday in those years. Watch the 'Bobby' who has stretched white gloves across his hands in a mark of authority. He is fascinatingly adept as he controls an avalanche of cyclists coming at him from all directions and weaving their way across deadly tramlines and between slow moving cart horses. Their dexterity in avoiding the myriad clumps of horse droppings, and countering every shift of the wheel in front as it fights for the smoothest passage along the wet cobblestones is hypnotising.

All these to-ings and fro-ings, home to work, then work to home would rarely take one outside the valley. We were very much a closed society, and it is difficult now to imagine the comparative isolation of the day. We did not feel it, we knew little difference. On recollection it was a transitional period in time, when the radio, or wireless as we knew it was then in its infancy. Television, but a utopian dream.

Films were in existence and most families went off to the 'pictures' once a week. And to make things really exciting, the 'talkies' were just coming about. Indeed the entire spectrum of life in the early 20's bore no resemblance to that of modern Britain.

Employment in the valley centred around the cotton mills, the shoe and slipper factories, and railway, whilst pastimes were varied. There was the inevitable fish and chip shop and the pubs, indeed a predominance of these. The Liberal club, second only to the 'con' club was the mecca for ballroom dancing and the 'Kings', following the closure of the 'Cosy', our Waterfoot cinema. Chapels were many, many more than there were churches. The one my own family attended was Bethesda, a fine building that has now disappeared.

But it was the 'Socials' and the Sunday 'rambles' across the moors that stand out so clearly in my mind. These 'get togethers' as with 'music evenings' when we all gathered around someone's piano for a sing-song were the very essence of a community spirit now extinct.

Next in order of delight came the train excursions to Blackpool, Morecambe, Southport, New Brighton or Holingworth Lake. All these wonders jump into crystal clear focus as I turn my mind back to the year of 1926.

CHAPTER 2

SCHOOL BOOTS

Sharp indeed are these early recollections. Most vivid perhaps is my earliest. It was the day that father loosened the buckle of his belt, and that strap, viewed from my innocent little eyes was all of four inches wide, and enormously thick. Not that he was about to use it, or even ever did; the mere threat was enough. Sufficient warning that anti social behaviour could manifest itself rapidly into the execution of summary justice.

It was the day when presumably half the housewives of Fairfield Avenue chose to peer out above their half netted windows and observe this little mite merrily urinating into his seaside bucket. Along with a suitable mixture of clay and dust, the whole preparation was destined for the manufacture of mud pies; what I took to be a quite legitimate pastime. These wives, however, as with the majority of Edwardian ladies, were 'not amused', and promptly advised mother of this blatant pornographic display. She in turn felt it her duty to inform father on his return from the office and hence the warning. The very threat of corporal punishment is ever the deterrent; I have never 'flashed' since that day, at least not in public!

That sordid event. and the day I was dragged almost through the very rollers of the kitchen mangle by the ends of a mop of curly red hair are among my earliest memoirs. Of the latter episode, I remember clearly my mother's frail arms winding away laboriously at the huge cast iron wheel that turned the wooden rollers. She seemed to be enduring a pitiful struggle as she endeavoured to wring out the very last particle of water from that monstrous blanket; and I only stood on tip toe to see if I could help!

To a child, every day brings some new excitement, never does the monotony or boredom rear its ugly head. There is always a new adventure waiting around the corner. In that particular year we moved to the other end of the avenue. This was really something; it was to a house with a sitting room no less, and what made the move doubly interesting to me was the fact that but a few doors away lived a little girl my own age, and who, like myself sported a head of fine red, curly hair. We were an immediate match. We walked hand in hand to school from the first day. Down Prospect Street, along Todd Carr Road up to the Pack Horse and through the 'Ginnel' to Thornfield where the council school stood. Together we explored the anatomical variations of male and female, and even at that immature age had carried out almost every pedagogy to be gleaned from the Kamasutra by the time we were six years old. She shall remain nameless!

On the whole, life at school was enjoyable, but the day to day happenings on our compact estate perched high on the valley slopes overlooking the River Whitewell and across to Seat Naze and the stone beacon circle was a utopia on its own. No-one was a stranger, you knew everyone by name.

What we would consider momentous happenings, transpired all the time. Perhaps the excited call when a rare aeroplane was heard and a whole gang of us would rush outside to watch it drone slowly overhead..... two wings held together with what appeared to be a mass of string netting; every time the engine coughed you wondered if it would fall from the sky. The Ice Cream vendor. Traditionally an Italian coming along the avenue, his gaudily painted cart pulled by a pathetic looking horse whilst he bellows out his ''ice'a cream'a'' and at the same time ring a huge hand bell with gusto. If you were fortunate enough to get down to Rawtenstall where the roads were a little less fearsome, you may glimpse the Wall's 'Stop me and Buy One' tricycle. Pedalling that monstrosity would earn the rider every penny he was paid.

Rawtenstall, although but as little as two miles away down the valley, was somewhat an upper class town to we natives of the upper reaches, Its wider streets not only boasted the presence of the town hall, but in the centre, there were two cinemas and the theatre. Sadly the latter fell into disuse around the thirties, along with the tram shed.

Back along our avenue few, if any motor cars passed during a whole day. An apple box would suffice for a set of wickets and the youngest players jacket or cap for a bowling mark, and a good days cricket was in the offing. I recall an occasion when an isolated trader did have the nerve to interrupt the game and I flung my bat in disgust into someone's garden. Unfortunately, my aim was high and my strength a little beyond expectation. It went clean through our neighbour's window and resulted in a tirade of abuse from both the irate neighbour and my father. He it was, who had to purchase the glass and re-glaze the offending gap. The lesson did me no harm however, I learned quite young the uses of putty, glasscutter and chisel.

A vision of that very stretch of Fairfield Avenue brings horse droppings to mind. These steaming heaps of gardeners gold became an obsession to some. Gold you really would think it was, with the acquirable value set by some of the neighbours. It was a crafty game of Olympic proportion to mount the steps two at a time, shovel in one hand and brush in the other and beating one and all in the headlong rush to be the first to stake claim to a treasured pile of steaming fresh dung. On occasion, I nearly had my head kicked in by an indignant donator whose patience was being sorely tried. From careful observation over a period of time, it was noted that when Mr. Ropers, the coalman, and his team of four rested, their nose bags were put into place and it was an ideal time to prepare for action; it was as if a conveyor belt had been switched on.... oats in at one end, and manure for the rhubarb churned out at the other.

When not engaged in sport of that nature, it could well be a game of ''Bully Bowels' was in process. This mysteriously named gadget comprised of a circular rolled metal ring, to which a metal arm was loosely suspended. Holding this arm you get the three feet diameter ring into motion by running pell mell along the road, bouncing it from kerb to kerb. There was a certain art in steering this rather primitive amusement but nevertheless it kept us all fit and out of mischief; or so one would assume. Racing down 'Walshes Brow', across Crabtree Avenue and down to Taylor Avenue was great stuff, particularly if you were one of the fortunate who had taken possession of a rare motor car tyre, and a big stick. Imagine our wanton mirth when 'big headed' Billie Hargreaves lost control of his recently acquired treasure. He couldn't keep up to the bouncing menace in his best Sunday clogs as it careered down the 'Tip' towards Globe Mill, where someone there gave it a passing kick and it swung sideways to bounce up the steps and straight through the chip shop door.

For a week or two we all stayed clear of that spot. A pity because that was where the river ran under Birtwistles Mill and an ideal position to throw stones at the multitude of rats that infested the waters. The little bridge over the sluiceway at Joe Churnsides nonetheless proved equal, and the sport continued.

But what of the 'One man bands'. They frequented our towns with a regularity. They were a sign of the times; A sad monument to the aftermath of war and impending unemployment. But in our innocent minds they were a phenomenon. We stared in amazement at the man, usually deformed to the extent of a missing arm or leg, half blind, or otherwise mutilated on the battle fields of northern France. He would have pushed his equipment along the road balanced precariously between a couple of old bicycle wheels, set up his base drum and treadle, his seat and the harmonica rest, and now he would grab his ukulele and burst forth in a cavalcade of musical contortion, 'Roses of Picardy', 'If you were the only girl in the world', 'Pack up your troubles' and any other tune popular at the time. It was all so riveting, yet with a hint of poignancy. We threw our pennies into the tin mug pinned to his ex army greatcoat and read the card proclaiming him an unemployed ex soldier. A hero for sure; back from the war to end all wars, and now a strike bound Britain, heading for a slump to end all slumps!

Yet like any little boy of today we saw none of the implications of gun worship. We carried our 'six' guns and repeaters, filled them with 'caps' which you could buy by the reel, or loose. With three or four of these little red wonders screwed into a miniature imitation of a mills bomb quite an explosion could be the happy result when thrown against the school wall under the teachers room..... But beware of Mrs. Chadwick! Her cane was shorter than regulation and she wielded it like a demon possessed. Or so we considered. Frankly, I preferred the 'slipper' across the backside, a standard punishment meted out to miscreants of my calibre in the senior school. I did not go short, and when Mrs. Ingham, all of fifty inches across the bust, put me over her knew for a spanking, the whole class was in a state of almost uncontrolled hilarity. Surely she was suffering more than I.

To all events however, Mr. Howarth, headmaster of my junior establishment gave me a glowing report when the time came to seek my path into the adult world. It is one I still possess, and however I came to climb so high in his assessments, the mystery remains. In particular having had me stand alongside him at the piano, and make me repeat some incongruous lyrics to the 'Ashgrove' that he had overheard me mimicking from the back of the class; and only the same week having received a report to the effect that I had been observed lying in the long grass alongside the school with the head girl! In modern parlance, I suppose we could have been said to be practising 'horizontal jogging'. He was not amused.

Decidedly, school in general did nothing to create a personal magnetism. Indeed, for several years I seemed to see little of it. With unremitting regularity, I went from one to each of the ten current illnesses; whooping cough, measles, chicken pox, pneumonia. scarlet fever, tonsillitis and finally, the killer of the day, diptheria. I got the lot! On what was expected to be my very last night, I recall a sea of faces peering down from around the bed; a doctor, a district nurse, mother, father and a host of anxious relations. My young brother Cyril, but a baby had been sent off to our grandparents. Nevertheless, one and all it seems were astounded. It seems I possess an inborn gift of survival. It has been an ally on many an occasion since.

Allowing myself to further languish in childhood nostalgia the very image of candles in jam jars, bulls eye torches, oil lamps and storm lamps, rickers made from rib bones we cadged from the butcher and polished to perfection. Collar studs and spats; clog irons that could shower a brilliant stream of sparks when you understood the right angle to bring your foot down against the kerbstone. All these come to mind.

A lone motor car parked along the avenue. It was sure to be the doctor. We always knew when someone was ill. He was one of the chosen few that possessed the status symbol.

But Fairfield Avenue! To me it will be forever synonymous with the Rees family. And they would in the end have the biggest impact on my life. Our two families had forged a close relationship as far back as strangers together arriving in the valley during the immediate 14-18 post war period.

Gladys, the eldest of the children became a staunch rider in the Rossendale Wheelers during the thirties and Fred, second eldest my very close friend, and eventual brother-in-law, whilst Dorothea, youngest at the time would be my future wife. The bond our parents cemented remains strong to this day.

Perhaps it was due to the Rees's origins having roots in the far rolling hills of Carmarthenshire, and my father's aloofness, stemming from managerial isolation that found both our families averse to their offsprings wearing the traditional clogs. Throughout industrial Lancashire the practice was habitual. It had sprung from a necessity on the flagstone floors of the cotton mills, but times were changing.

If there is something you haven't got, and another child has, then the absence becomes all the more tantalising.

So Fred and I found ourselves sitting on the kerbside, quite often looking the picture of dejection as our pal Joe White clumped up to us in HIS

brightly polished clogs. Joe was a hefty lad; we called him fat. So the
noise He could make as he strode along caused even more yearning to
at least try a pair on. After many attempts there came the day when Joe
succumbed to temptation. I believe it was a halfpenny, or a stick of P.K.
spearmint he was promised, but it worked and I walked, or rather
waddled down 'Walshes Brow' nearly falling head over heels in the
process.
Predictably, it was the 'little things' that gave most joy to we children of
the time. There were few toys in those less affluent days but we were as
happy as any child of today. If we couldn't afford the latest craze, a Yo-
Yo, then we would spend many a happy hour aping our elders. Tying
spotted handkerchiefs round a pudding basin and carrying it by the reef
knot; perhaps sloshing cold tea about in the blue enamel 'Billie Can' like
all the mill workers carried to work. And how the girls loved to drape their
head and shoulders in a black shawl and pretend they were off to the mill.
In the early dark evenings, we could spy on old Nelly Openshaw nipping
craftily through the side door of the 'White Horse' with her quart jug and
then sneaking back home with her ration of 'Old Tom' ale. Little Johnny
Banham, the bowlegged concertina player from the Salvation Army
band would come in for some uncomplimentary mimicking as well. He
made such a great show, and then when the crowd was pulled he lost no
time in dashing around with his little red velvet collecting bag suspended
on the end of a long stick. But it was his little legs that made everything
so funny as he ran in and out between the watchers then invariably
tripped over something and fell into the drummer or cornet player and
threw everyone out of tune.
Like any other town, Waterfoot had its thriving market. Millar Barn Lane
and surroundings would be a hive of activity on every Friday, all because
in those days, very few people would have either the inclination or the
means to shop outside their own locality. So after helping mother carry
home the laden wicker baskets and oilskin bags, I would be awarded a
penny piece and told to, spend it as I please. The choices were several;
it would buy two separate ha'penny bags of toffees, two packets of
chewing gum, a roll of caps or a pennyworth of chips. It was the latter
I invariably chose, not due to an insatiable passion for the fried potato,
but for the immense pleasure I drew from watching the passage of the
invincible 'spud' from the hand of Mr. Entwistle, through the 'chipper'
and into the bucket below.

Having returned to the market, probed every stall both on the outside and in the hall, then through the big shed that Jack Harvey leased, nothing better could be found to spend my penny on so into Burnley Road it was time to go. To place your back on the wall and watch the queue from inside the chip shop. When the time was ripe, in I would go, last in a long line with ample time and a good position to view the miraculous chipping of a whole bucketful of freshly peeled potatoes. The last half will go into the fryer, Mrs. Entwistle will take over and along will come Mister. Total methodical magic. Left hand loosely holding on end a ready peeled potato, and right hand bringing down the long metal arm as the left returns with practised dexterity for the next victim. Into the white enamelled bucket below cascaded an almost continuous shower of symmetrically square chips from the grid above. After I'd shaken the salt and vinegar onto my little feast and left the shop behind, I considered it a penny very well spent. If Jimmy Savile was to ever ask ME what I would like 'fixed', then that would be it; just to pull down that handle, even if there was but only one potato available.

A high level of importance must have been placed in those days on the insistence that all items of a hygienic nature must be finished white. Enamel buckets, plates, cups, pans, paper bags that held food stuffs including the cornet shaped bags that held our pennyworth of sweets, all were white, and even the doorsteps. These were scrubbed daily to perfection and the edges finished off with 'donkey stone' which was exchanged for woollens from the rag and bone man. Anything that could breed germs had to be cut short. That brings me to the subject of our barber Squire Grimshaw. 'Squire' I think, had been an army officer or more likely a sergeant major; perhaps he was an ex Prussian lancer, for lance he certainly was well known for. Never was he short of a customer, for it was the day when fashion dictated 'short back and sides'. If it didn't come off with the scissors then the hand operated shears would remove it, sometimes in a whole tuft at a time! There would be no 'nits' in OUR hair when HE had finished, and to give him his due, he was motivated by modern trends; he had a wax taper and matches and when all else failed he would give you a 'singe'. I remember well going along with Fred Rees and his little brother David who we called 'Midge'. Young David, only about three years of age shot out of his chair screaming his head off as Squire lit up his taper. His flamboyance lost him THAT little customer for a time to come.

Seventy years later, it is interesting to note the shop is still a hairdresser's, though it is doubtful that a rack of pipes will be on display for the discerning smoker, the cheaper of which were cherry wood at two pence each and the clay ones at one penny. Then along from there was a small counter from which he would serve you with a plug of twist for tuppence, a packet of Woodbines for the same price or an ounce of 'Players' pipe tobacco for less than a shilling. This all sounds very cheap, until we recall a man's wage then averaged a mere two pounds a week.

Consistent with this trend for an increased awareness of hygienic living it became noticeable that public house 'tap rooms' were absenting themselves of the sawdust lined spittoons. Tram operators were at last able to remove their offensive "No Spitting" notices. The penalty had been £5, a matter of at least two week's wages, and at a time when penalties were carried out to the letter.

The old habit of chewing tobacco and 'pinching' snuff was dying fast. Packaged cigarettes, Woodbines, Star, Park Drive, Capstain, B.D.V. with the coupons, and 'Kensitas', with the little packet on the end and 'four for your friends' were becoming commonplace.

To my little mind, it was not of particular note, but to the older generation the changing times held a deep significance. The impact of radio was tremendous; of films, recorded music, the motor car, and now the aeroplane. In a matter of ten to fifteen years a whole way of life was revolutionised.

In an unheralded wave of enthusiasm around the mid twenties, father flung all and everything of little consequence from a chest of drawers in the living room and in went every conceivable component necessary in the assembly of a wireless. There are coils and condensers, valves and speakers. Hundreds of screws and endless masses of wire.

I remember huge soldering irons poking out of the kitchen fire and solder spilt on the linoleum. Of course, there was the accumulator that had to be recharged at the shop once a week and earphones I had to put on and listen carefully for some crackling voice called Daventry National. The earphones were made of steel and Bakelite and it was all I could do to hold them on my head without overbalancing and falling off the chair. I think I enjoyed it all much more when in later years, we were able to merely plug into the wall and turn a switch. Much more fun I thought was to wind up the new gramophone and put on a record of Sandy Powell, even if it meant changing the steel needle every time.

All these indoor activities, like playing with the clockwork Hornby train, which never seemed to work as well after increasing affluence saw us putting a carpet over the oilcloth, and 'snakes and ladders' and 'Ludo' were all very well when it was wet or cold. But out in the open was where we lads found our greatest amusements. Just everyday happenings, that was enough.

Perhaps the scissors grinder was coming along. The shower of sparks was what we were waiting for. First he would stop his bicycle, then drop down a metal support in order to raise the back wheel from the road and pedal merrily away whilst a belt attached to a grindstone on the handlebars set the whole operation into motion. A good quarter of an hour he would spend sharpening scissors, knives and garden shears.

After he had gone, it may be the turn of the milkman. Abel Heap the farmer. He was a canny old devil who had a knack of roping us all in to help with the 'hay making' without parting with so much as a sixpence. We watched him carefully as he ladelled out the milk into a waiting housewife's jug. He never spilt a drop as his gill or pint measure dipped in and out of the churn. When the horse reared a little in the shafts of his two wheeled cart, we felt sure that one day the leather straps holding in the churns would break and give us the thrill of watching twenty gallons of milk spew across the road.

But we were never so lucky.

Next week, it may be the turn of the steam roller. That was really something. It was the next best thing to nipping down to the railway goods yard and watching the shunting engines clattering wagons about. When the steam roller arrived along would come that massive horse drawn cauldron with a fire burning underneath to melt the tar. And more horses and carts full of chippings. Men with big shovels to spread the stone and others carrying cans with large spouts to spread the tar. This would be a great day, an entire day, because we could follow along all three avenues. If we didn't get too close to the men, who would likely take a calculated swipe at us with their shovels, we could dip our boots into the soft tar and then some chippings. And so another exciting day would close.

More than any other factor; modes of transport, forms of entertainment or the changing world of commerce, etc. I consider the changes of attitude towards authority, courtesy, and the general sense of care within the community, as our greatest source of concern in the closing years of the twentieth century.

At the point of time I write about, there was never the need or even the concern to turn the key, or press home the bolt of the door at night. At least, not in our town. An unlocked or an open door was ever an invitation to step over the threshold. The neighbours would pop in any time.

Had you had need to seek the services of the local 'bobby' there existed none of the apprehension we see today. He had respect for you, as you had for him. If we as children, erred, then we expected a dressing down, or even a 'clip round the ear'hole' if the severity of our misdemeanour warranted it. It is doubtful the incident would then justify the tedious completion of half a dozen of our contemporary blight, the eternal 'form'. Neither would it be reported to father, nor any conceivable civil rights organisation. We accepted rough justice for what it was and got on with the business of enjoying ourselves.

In marked contrast too, was the esteem of the soldier and the sailor. Arriving home on leave, his immaculate uniform pressed to perfection and the regimental badge, buttons and boots a calculation to turn anyone's eye. There was little necessity to hide the King's uniform in order to evade a terrorist's bullet. Along with the police, he was a mark of accepted law abidance.

Then again, all was convention, acceptability of a lifestyle that did nothing to cause the scargilistic anarchism of the late twentieth century. Manners were of a high priority, good ones, and those of a caring nature were taught both at home and in the schools. As instance the process of even walking along the pavement. A boy was taught to walk along the kerbside of his mother, or any other female; to doff, or at least touch the nib of his cap when greeting a lady. When a funeral procession was passing to stop and remove one's hat. At the dining table, to refrain from lifting a knife and fork until your parents did and not to speak unduly out of course, should company be present.

In all perhaps life was a little more formal.

Certainly there was less variety in the spread of a British meal table in that day. You little thought of expressing undue emotion at the eternal servings of sago or tapioca puddings, or the fruits of the day, and every day, prunes or apples; laced with custard.

Plenty of bacon dripping to keep out the cold and drink as much milk as the purse allowed. These were the theories, and if we lacked a fair percentage of vitamins, then a spoonful of cod liver oil or if you were

lucky, a forage into the wax tub of Virol. At all times, remember you're British. That was of dire consequence when the need to scream out in pain afflicted a little mite; as the neat iodine dripped into an open wound the stiff upper lip syndrome decreed the toddler bite deep onto his tongue, draw even more blood, hold back any suggestion of a cowardly tear, and hopefully not collapse in the true cause of British impassivity. With all this Edwardian conformity safely ensconced beneath my little blue cap, and a leather school bag dangling from my shoulder whilst threatening to trip me up at every step, I set out to the council school at the tender age of four and a half years. Father said the extra mile walk would do me no harm as at the nearby church school, there was every chance of religious bias. Today, I believe it is political, though be that as it may, I understood none of these things. Only the ability to enjoy every minute of the day was our concern; and in retrospect, that we did. On the periphery of our mixed class playground, I recall the comparatively low wall that hid from sight the row of toilet cubicles for the use of all the children, and at the same time supported the flat grey slate that acted as the boys urinal. Like all little boys anxious to demonstrate their superiority in some silly little game a select few of us took up the challenge of this six foot barrier to see who could be first to 'clear the top'. By a deft application of thumb and forefinger a jet which would defy all the laws of gravity would ensue and one of us would take the honours as first to pee over the top. This was all very well, and most of the girls appeared to think the display quite amusing but one fine day, a tot of a more parochial outlook took exception to the display and reported us to 'Miss'. She, as expected, took umbrage and determined to catch out the miscreants. It happened that her timing was impeccable; but her path was disastrous! The course she took as she strode along the playground found her running parallel to the particular wall at the most inopportune moment and despite a brilliant blue and cloudless sky, 'Miss' discovered a certain vapour in the air. She burst around the corner livid, to use but a mild adjective, and was then confronted by the four of us in full spate and encouraged to greater heights by a mixed group of ardent supporters...... That was the end of that little sport. On reassembly of the class, the guilty four of us were paraded to the front, where we each received 'six of the best' across the palm of the hand, a regulation maximum with the standard cane I believe.
That pastime was out, but there were others; marbles, pop alleys, hop

scotch, and countless more. And Christmas was to be remembered every year for the traditional break with routine class work. A week or so before break there were decorations to glue together, long chains of assorted tissue paper and then yule tide drawings to paint and pin all over the walls. But the real excitement came the last day before we vacated the school. It was the annual distribution of a multitude of free gifts, all bearing the name of some local trader or a national distributor. There were the Oxo painting books, and a host of other useful commodities; crayons, pencils, India rubbers, calendars, books of arithmetic tables and balloons, all depicting the merits of Horlicks, Ovaltine, Frys chocolate, Bisto and Lifeboy carbolic soap. The most fascinating item, and which I've kept all these years, was a polished wooden ruler bearing the name of Marshalls of Burnley. As with present day rulers, it displayed the imperial measure to one edge and metric on the other. I refer to 1927 of course, and when teacher handed these round she explained the significance and advantages of the metric system, told us that next term we would be taught the rudiments which were quite simple and metrication would shortly follow. Indeed, we did learn, but sixty five years later, I still await the elusive day.

Asked to specify a particularly favourite day in a long calendar of outdoor festivities, it would be difficult. These were pre-television days and constantly some amateur event appeared to be in progress weekly in one or other of the local towns. But Empire Day was the crowning day for processions and carnival. The huge parade of Boy Scouts, Boys brigade, British Legion, local territorial soldiers and all the valleys 'prize' bands was endless; Irwell Springs, Goodshaw, Haslingden and Water, all banging away on gaily painted drums whilst others tried to blow their guts out. Between the bands and at strategic intervals came the brilliant floats with tableaus depicting colonial every day life. Indian maharajas and the tea pickers of Ceylon; and we waved our paper Union Jacks with a gusto that would surely keep the British Empire intact for eternity. The coloured faces did credit to a hard working mother. It would be hard to find a coloured skin in the surrounds of Rossendale during the early parts of this century. A tin of black or brown 'Cherry Blossom', at times aided with a touch of lard and a handful of soot from up the chimney would suffice. Of historical note, it may be added that the only 'black man' I ever saw prior to the outbreak of war was the great Leary Constantine, professional cricketer for Nelson C.C. who made regular appearances when the team played Rawtenstall in the Lancashire League. In post war years, Constantine became a man of note on the scene of Jamaican politics.

I am thankfully gifted with a mind of photographic clarity and though not of any immense importance, it is sometimes nice to relax in nostalgic bliss and allow a kaleidoscope of memorabilia cross the frontiers of subconsciousness. To see again the hardwood desks with their folding seat to accommodate two pupils, the two stained ink wells made of white pottery and nestled in the appropriate holes; the grooved inset and the narrow beading that held back your ink pen and pencils from sliding down across your exercise books. The blotting paper that seemed in constant use, and the bright metal pencil holder you were expected to use in order to obtain the last half inch of valuable lead in the County Council's 'HB's'. A halfpenny stick of 'Spanish' to suck, or a pomegranate to be picked at with an unhygienic pin on the way home from school. There would be Mr. Roper's coal cart, fully loaded and hauled by a team of four smartly groomed horses. All resplendent in their brass refinery. Would they make it to the top of Prospect Street without a slip on the wet cobblestones? Then coming down with two of the horses acting 'brakeman'; would there be need of the wooden sprigs to scotch the wheels of a potential runaway? A runaway of a different nature we had recently had on this very hill. It was the newly inaugurated bus service, and the brakes on this single deck bus had failed three quarters of the way up. As it careered back, the driver miraculously swung round the back end and wedged the vehicle over the chasm that ran the length of the rear of Bethseda Chapel.

In these visions, I see rapidly changing modes as the impact of Hollywood dictates the new fashions. Fast disappearing is the man's 'flat cap' to be replaced by the gangster style trilbies, with a drooping brim to half shield one eye, and a cigarette dangling in the corner of the mouth to complete the image.

As we boys craftily edge along a row of Victorian 'back to backs' we take imaginary bets on who will be first to kick the coal chute cover back over the hole as the coalman deftly swings his sack across his shoulder and lands a hundredweight of coal neatly along the pavement. Then it's who can run the fastest!

And run we would on a Wednesday; straight home from school to be greeted by the luscious aroma of home cooked bread. Yesterday the

entire fireplace and range would have been blackleaded, and the brass
work polished to perfection, fire irons, fender and the lot. Would I get
home before my brother and be first to taste those scrumptious muffins
and the 'oonbottoms' that were my favourites. Along with the tin loaves
and cobs, it was always a mystery to me why they were all laid out in
long rows along the hearth. But so it was, and when all was cleared away,
it was my little job to rake all the coals back from under the oven and back
into the main fire which had been allowed to die down.

Monday was traditionally washing day. It had to be a specific day as
more than often the whole streets would be festooned with overflowing
clothes lines slung from side to side and no tradesman stood a chance of
getting his cart through on that day. Due to inclement weather on one
occasion, mother had loaded the indoor clothes rack to a dangerous
capacity. The load included some heavy wet blankets which were all but
still dripping, and the trouble with these monstrosities was that they were
suspended from the ceiling by a couple of hooked pulleys and operated
by a rope that on occasion could be suffering from an invisible display
of wear and tear. So ours was on that day. Even the stoutest has its limits
and cares little in choosing a more opportune moment to end its career.
With a sickening crack it plummeted down, upending the remnants of a
half cleared tea table and depositing its entire load over my brother, who
up to that moment had been sat unconcernedly in a new enamel bath tub.
Why is it that fathers are rarely around when these catastrophes occur?
Father was around the following week however. It was he that suggested
we paper the ceiling. I think they wrote that famous ditty in his honour.
After a total fiasco witnessing mother, brother, father and myself
balancing on chairs, boxes or whatever else was available, and supporting a careering sheet of slimily pasted wallpaper with brooms and long
mops, the venture into professional decorating was abandoned.

Possibly the vibrations ensuing from repeated thuds on the ceiling were
the cause of next weeks calamity; the saga of the dreaded sash cord.
These cords are held in boxed housing on either side of the window frame
and support a heavy cast iron weight that holds the upper frame in its
suspended position. The said cords, although manufactured in a high
grade twine have a limited life, and when frayed and worn unseen by the
naked eye they snap, heaven help the unfortunate soul that has his hands
or fingers resting on the sill three feet below. The science is to understand
the tilt if one side has already broken and counteract the impending

danger by a hasty repair before the second one follows suit. Be that as it may; it hadn't been done when the furniture salesman's ladder was rested against the bedroom window where we were to have a new wardrobe pulled through. Needless to say, it wouldn't take the bend in the narrow stairs; there seemed to be a prevailing habit of making extra wide furniture, and frustratingly shrivelled staircases. That was the position then as father lowered the rope to the man on the ground. Whilst he did his work with that, Dad rested his hands on the sill and contemplated how to remove the rest of the frame. The analysis concluded then in six seconds flat. Down crashed the hardwood frame, complete, until a split second before the impact with two panes of heavy glass, and raked every finger and thumb from left to right.

Normally his attitude to adversity was remarkably constrained. He was a calm and undemonstrative person by nature, but on this occasion all hell was let loose. There were words I never knew existed, at least not in father's acceptable code of dialogue. Mother played a low profile, but brought lint, iodine and bandages, whilst we kids helped sweep up the glass and prayed the rope that would pull up the dreaded wardrobe held in one piece.

To escape minor domestic upheaval of this nature, it was always possible by devious means to suggest a counterpoise. Could one help with the shopping for instance? Holding the wicker basket in anticipation usually worked, probably a loaf was required, so it was off up to the Co-op on the top road. Fred Beardsworth was the manager of this little gold mine on Edgside Road. He was the man who never appeared to take money from anyone; he just wrote it all down in a little blue book, when we asked for a cardboard box he was ever obliging. These boxes then found their way to the scree that tumbled from the top road to the field below and we all called it modestly, 'the slide'. They were broken down into squares which virtually became sledges, because without that valuable piece of cardboard there would soon be a hole in your breeches and then watch out when you got indoors.

Winters gave excellent scope for intuition. There were admirable slopes on our hillsides for sledging and the days when you went into a shop to buy a sledge were far away. No; long before the snow arrived, hands were busy seeking apple boxes and the like; though the wood was somewhat of a curse as it split and splintered, the strip steel bands would make excellent runners, and two pieces of tapering wood for the sides and four pieces of 6" x 18" for the top, a few nails and a length of stout string and an instrument of sound proportion was in the offing. I do sometimes believe we had more fun, anticipating the fun!

By and large, summer days seemed endless. They had a compelling quality. A visit to Uncle Tom's at Lancaster could be the highlight of any boy's dream. What more could a child crave? Trips on the River Lune or along the Lancaster Canal in 'rich uncle's' very own boat. I really assumed him a millionaire. There were outings to Morecambe and to the rocky coast at Silverdale, but best of all there were the visits to Lancaster railway station to see the new L.M.S. expresses steaming through at 80 miles an hour and setting up new record breaking runs to Scotland. These occasions were destined to have a dramatic effect on my later life. Returning home by train and stopping at such big stations as Preston and Manchester Victoria, my small eyes boggled at the sheer wonder of it all. Travel was already stirring my wanderlust yearnings, and Dad saw it. Be patient were his words; soon you'll be eight years old and in the cubs, then to camp you'll go and that will be really living.

So as yet, it was home entertainments. May Day and Whitsuntide spent watching the girls dancing around the Maypole or taking part in the fabulous walks that commemorated these pagan and christian occasions. Mothers would vie for the honour of producing the prettiest of dresses and the most gorgeous of flower baskets for the girls whilst we could tease them over their frilly knickers, or their navy blue E.T.B.'s that showed below their frocks.

Car outings were naturally non-existent, but we had the train, and whereas the tram was restricted to comparatively flat roads and within town limits, buses were now entering the scene, to give a more attractive door to door service and a wider scope. So it cannot be said we lived in isolation any longer. I enjoyed many trips down to Grandad's drapery shop in Ramsbottom and in particular, to Aunty Polly's. At my grand-parents, it was the ever intriguing rocking chairs that failed to upend when I tried my damnest to make them do so; cane chairs that left ridges on your bottom and broken pieces that stuck through my pants; flagstone floors and a shallow stone sink, whilst upstairs was a big iron bedstead with huge brass knobs and a handle to tighten up the springs. Outside at the bottom of the yard was the 'privy' containing an earth bucket which the council men emptied every week. I recall Auntie's was a much more modern affair; but it was a little frightening; across the yard, through a red painted door I would only go when nature offered its last chance. On the dreaded bench with the gaping hole defying the circumference of my little bottom, I would sit trembling. Then at the precise moment of balance, the loaded bucket, pivoted on a metal rod six feet below and seeming to me to be down by the very gates of hell, would upend, with an almighty crash, and echoing terrible vibrations it resounded through every atom of my frail little body. I did wish they had a W.C. like ours with a nice long chain to pull. At times, I wonder how ever my trembling fingers reached the neat squares of newspaper strung on the wall.

And when I got home, I would tell father about the large stone sarsaparilla bottle that Grandad used for a hot water bottle, it was just like ours. But perhaps that's where he got the idea in the first place!

Despite the thrills and excitement of going off to some relation or other, home was home, and it was always nice to return to the valley. After all, as an instance nowhere else did they have brass bands as good as ours. Probably because nowhere else would they have generated the rivalry that existed in these smaller communities. And wasn't there the challenge from across the hills; the land they called Yorkshire. With a gusto unbelievable, practice hours seemed endless with Goodshaw, Water, Haslingden and Irwell Springs all aiming to better the likes of the Black Dyke Mills or Brighouse and Rastrick. Every other household it seemed, had at least one member of the family blasting out on a euphonium, a trumpet, an oboe or horn. And if not that, then a set of drums would set every cat and dog in the street howling for pity. Mother said the only time there was peace was when they were all shut up together in the solid stone practice rooms; and even then she suffered torments, dreading that the Salvation Army would come round banging on the big brass drum to fill the gap.

So that was my entertainment; my way of life. A happy existence enriched now by the prospect of a venture into scouting. From primary school to junior school and now the big hands of the clock looked down on an impatient little eight year old, eager to see outside the bounds of his native Lancashire.

CHAPTER 3

CUB BOOTS

In terms of pure membership, my association with the Scout movement was to last a mere eight years, but on reflection what a tremendous impact those few years were to have upon an entire lifestyle, and over future decades.

The predominant effect of its influence, apart from having moulded a more caring citizen, was the lifetime's enjoyment I was to derive from an extremely close affinity to the countryside.

First, as a wolf cub would come the essentials of scouting practice; the golden rule of 'a good deed for the day', and to accomplish this without the slightest thought of financial reward. In fact, we were taught to stubbornly refuse any coppers that may be offered as inducement to help anyone, even in the slightest of ways. Secondly, we had to learn the necessity of good organisation and the true interpretation of the slogan, 'Be Prepared'. After that it was tying and untying a multitude of various knots, the rudiments of first aid and basic cooking.

Taking into account the fact that much of this early training in overcoming 'tenderfoot' status was held in the classrooms of my junior school, and in rooms where I had taken a few whacks from Mrs. Chadwick's evil cane, the week we all had to report for camp preparation came only too soon.

On the great day, we lined up outside St. Anne's Church. Kit bags, some as large as us, and threatening to pull us over backwards were thankfully flung up onto Ridhalgh's lorry and then we all leapt aboard to set out for Sawley. It was Whitsuntide, 1931.

Swanside beck, where camp was set up lies under the shadow of Pendle Hill, that dominant rise commanding the plains of lower Ribblesdale. Only recently father had walked me here, to the very summit and pointed below to the villages of Downham and Rimmington close to where the camp would be. In the distance, we picked out Ingleborough and Penyghent. Peaks that sent my blood racing in speculative wonder. But for now, the mystique would remain in embryo.

On arrival at Swanside, the picture was chaos, or so it seemed to us as we tripped over guy ropes attempting to erect the huge army bell tents,

fell over attempting to lift water carriers that must have seen service in the
Crimean War, and heaved logs, stones, cast iron 'dixies', ropes and
stakes, and a multitude of other paraphernalia that goes into establishing
a camp.
Total organisation reigned over the site by dusk nonetheless. Of course,
the scoutmaster knew it would. Cocoa was handed round in tin mugs and
the traditional camp fire sing song broke out. Then, at ten o'clock, it was
time to spend our very first night under canvas.
Of course, I tripped over the guy rope on the way into the tent, as did
everyone else. The knife, fork, spoon, enamel plate and mug were placed
above the pillow, which comprised of your kit bag stuffed with any spare
clothing you had, and then you slipped into bed. Bed being no less than
two army blankets fastened together with steel blanket pins and placed
on the hard ground with nothing between but a rubber ground sheet;
army issue again. In fact, just about everything one put a hand on bore
the government little arrow; the one that adorned a convict's clothes as
well.
But that mattered little. We were all exhausted by sheer hard work and
pure elation. Tonight we would all sleep well; or so it was imagined.....
It started with a competition as to who could kick each other the hardest,
and miss the centre pole at the same time. That is because in a bell tent
you all sleep like the hands of a clock, the twelve of us with heads at the
tent's perimeter and feet to the centre pole. That excitement died down
but must have attracted the attention of a herd of young bullocks who
considered sport could be had running round the tents, kicking all the guy
ropes and later leaving all their trademarks in the form of a symmetrical
circle of cow pats three feet outside the tent's verge. They probably
finished their antics by three in the morning but by then we all were
missing the luxury of the feather beds we had left behind, and letting every
one else know the fact. I think it was David Whittaker that suggested Pa
Chase's tip, and he was a real old scouter; so we all started digging under
where our hip bones were already making inroads in the terra firma and
found old 'Pa' was right; it really did help to induce sleep: all then were
on the very point of final inertia when the formidable shrill of a bugle all
but pierced our ear drums. It was known as 'reveille'; the call that tells
us it's time to waken up, and get up.
Joe White, I think, was the only one that had slept. He was the one that
wore clogs, but now like the rest of us he had to be shod in regulation

black pumps. But Joe was a clumsy lad and this morning he was still half
asleep when he staggered out of the tent, minus his pumps, and walked
straight into one of those circular 'pats' I mentioned..... His next move
took him straight down to the river.

Altogether it had not been the best of introductions to the joys of
communal living. Nevertheless, boys are boys, and fun will be found in
any situation, adverse or advantageous. By the time the bugle had
sounded 'cookhouse' and breakfast was over, it was time to 'break' the
union flag, have kit inspection and prepare for the day's walk with the
intrepid 'Pa' Chase. Once the thick dew had cleared we were away and
with his incalculable wealth of rural knowledge put to excellent benefit,
we lads one and all learned the code of the countryside, the names of the
wild flowers in the hedges and fields, the berries you could eat and those
you could not. The ways of the wild creatures and a compassion for all,
be they animal or human. He was the very essence of civilised humanity
and I feel we youngsters owe that individual a lot, for the dignity and
feeling that he instilled in us for later life.

For two more years we returned to the same field for the annual camp.
I enthused with so much fervour when at home that even father packed
up tent and belongings, and on more than one occasion, we caught the
train to Chatburn and walked the few miles to spend a happy weekend.
Rossendale's involvement with the movement, was considerable, and
came 'of age' in 1933. There was a big jamboree held on the football field
at Kirk, as the locals knew Newchurch, and among many other activities
of the day a message from the Chief Scout, Lord Baden Powell of Gilwell
was read out by the regional commissioner from the main stand. From
memory I imagine him a small man as all that comes to mind is an
enormous megaphone being held by an invisible person and threatening
to topple him over at any moment.

Two years later, and myself resplendent in full scouts uniform, the scene
had shifted to Scout Bottom, aptly named, where the 4th Rossendale
troop had its headquarters. Known as Hopkins Own, we understood it
so named due to a minor hitch in local ecclesiastical administration. Be
that as it may, it little concerned the likes of we gang of merry lads;
amongst us there were many denominations, Wesleyans, Baptists,
Church of England, Roman Catholic and even agnostics such as myself.
All were eager to get on with the business of scouting as depicted by
Baden Powell and to lean away from church parades, drum banging and

too close an affinity to matters in any way political.

The weekly 'scout night' never came round quickly enough. That room up the steps of the old mill by the river. Here competition was keen as together we struggled for honours; second class, first class, first aid badges, cooks badges and the like, and all with the object of finding ourselves one day to be chosen an aspiring patrol leader.

Next the final treat of the evening; a 'Beano' in the wooden hut 'chippie' at the bottom of Bridge Street. A tuppenny mixture which comprised of chips and mushy peas in a basin, laced well with salt and vinegar, and if you had been lucky to squeeze another penny from mother, a bottle of Bownesses pop.

It must be said the highlight, to a small band of chums that became inseparable, were however, the weekend, and the annual camps.

1935 saw us at Golborne, and the zenith of that week turned out to be the quelling of a hay stack fire which we had almost accomplished before the arrival of the fire brigade. After arriving back in camp as black as the ace of spades, we had the pleasure of being commended instead of scolded. In fact, the episode earned us an accolade from the fire officer and even a write up in the local newspaper.

Camping, and in some respects the very pull of the outdoors, or perhaps a desire to break away at any opportunity from the stability of accepted conformity became obsessional as the year 1936 progressed. It is known I believe as adolescence. And mine was to take an unorthodox course. This year would claim my fourteenth birthday, at that period in time it was a most significant anniversary. A point in life when you unpacked your school bag for the last time, and set out into the unknown world beyond.

Rather than frighten me, it was a fulfilment that had beckoned since first I crossed the yard at senior school.

In the light of today's thinking, fourteen years of age was an extremely immature time in life to set out on a path of self determination, career wise, or otherwise in the pursuit of adult concepts. In retrospect, this is not quite so. The mind of this young teenager, as with his even younger counterpart in Victorian times was extremely sharp; if not in academic terms, then in all surety with the ways of the immediate world around him. We witness now so often the mathematical and scientific geniuses that abound, yet invariably they could not inform you if Birmingham was to be north, or to the south of London.

In any event to me, it was a milestone. And with the great day looming, but no immediate sign of work having surfaced, I gave myself to a little reminiscing. Reflecting on the change in habits and in particular, the employment of young people may assist in formulating a pattern for my future. Hadn't father said over and over again, it was time to start taking life seriously, even at that tender age. Whilst the chosen few of wealthier parents had the privilege of extending their education until the age of sixteen, the mass of children were in the factory within a few days of their fourteenth birthday. This my parents did not want of me. Somehow they would find the funds needed for further education, but no, they had a stubborn son. What I wanted was to get out in the world and earn a living; to help contribute to the family maintenance, wasn't there a sister on the way now as well? Family allowances and the like were still a long way off.

Although it would take a world war and a virtual revolution in its aftermath to drastically close the doors on the Britain of post Edwardian times, there were nevertheless, changes taking place. Noticeable in abundance, as I looked back.

The old flat cap had all but disappeared, so too the tram with its slatted wood seats, and the horse hair seats in our local trains. Silent films were on their way out and the talkies taking over, so too the theatres and music halls were all falling into decay. Increasing everyday was motor traffic; buses, lorries and even a sprinkling of private cars, mostly owned by the professional and business classes. Cobblestones and tram lines that epitomised the Edwardian age were giving way to macadammed roads; here and there, on some steep hill, cobblestones remained by the kerbside to assist a weary carthorse haul a heavy load, their iron shod hooves making an impossible grip on treacherous asphalt. Trilbies, belts and American shirts, these were in, the braces out. Disappearing too were spats and men's suspenders, boys garters that held up a pair of loosely knitted school stockings as elasticated tops became popular. Though note could be taken of the fashion dictates of male influence, it ensured the retention of the female suspender, a highly significant sex symbol, for some considerable time to come.

And where was the ever dominant railway time table, threaded with string and hung on the hook behind the toilet door? That was now to be replaced by chromium plated holders and a clean white roll of expensive tissue paper. The horse troughs, once aflow with water a passing traveller would not deem undrinkable, now a crumbling monument to a bygone age, its water green and noxious. Tomorrow, in all probability, it will vanish in the wake of progress.

Ever increasing commercialisation too was erasing the desire, and probably the joy of originating and fabricating one's every day needs; the home baking of bread and cakes, the knitting and sewing of the family clothing. Even the porridge pan was to be neglected for the processed wheat of trans Atlantic enterprise. And gone was the need to mix flour and water for the dubious adhesive that would hopefully secure wallpaper to wall, or to stir lime and water to a paste in the bucket for ceilings and outbuildings. Now it was all coming ready mixed in tins.

However, there were still some time consuming hobbies left in a society fast turning to manufactured entertainments. Our fathers laboured away happily on treadle fretwork machines to produce admirable jigsaw puzzles, cigarette boxes, jewel boxes and marquetry pictures of an immense variety; and all from the plywood of discarded tea chests.

Somewhere around the age of ten I had outgrown the thrill of knocking on doors and running away; tying black thread to a door knocker and passing it over the gate to play up some unfortunate old soul; enjoying such games as 'Billie show thi lantern' or even taking little girls round the back of the fountains in Edgside Park to see how THEY were made. Even gathering up old pram wheels and fixing them to home made trollies was losing its appeal. But about this time Dad purchased a new gramophone, still of the wind up variety but nevertheless far more modern than the old phonograph I imagine he acquired at the same time as the wedding ring. Of particular enchantment was that this machine would play a full ten inch record without the need to rewind, although it was still necessary to sprint across the room and give a few turns if you wanted to hear the last few bars of Beethoven's Seventh Symphony in the tempo the genius first wrote it.

This gramophone was the agent that set me on a course of musical appreciation that would last into infinity; though I little knew it then. The presence of Schubert and Mozart amongst the likes of Jack Paine, Henry Hall, Al Bowly, Les Allen, Elsie Carlisle and Phyllis Robins perhaps accounted for this.

Dying another slow death was the annual pilgrimage to Holcombe Fair at easter. On this day the Brittania Coconutters, black faced and in traditional Morris costume danced the entire twelve miles from Bacup to

the ground on Holcombe Hill. But not dead, and far from it was Guy
Fawkes night, the fifth of November. Until I was old enough to know
better, our little gang warfares progressed. Stacks of wood, old furniture
and a prized motor tyre would change hands as we raided each others
hard sought collection, and every night for the preceding three weeks,
would be fraught with danger. Long poles and a handful of stones were
intended as a deterrent, but on occasion the defence, or raid could get
a little out of hand and blood would be spilt. I believe the essence of
cunning and counter espionage to be the prime motivation in all the
pleasure we derived. Was there material here for the psychologist? Were
any of us to be battlefield commanders? Whatever the answer, in my
mind the entire manoeuvres are stunningly clear; Raid and counter raid,
and then the final reckoning, when survey showed a heap of combustible
rubbish no larger than at the very outset. It had all been a wild but
wonderful three weeks and if anything, the fireworks and bonfire were
a mild consequence. And with certainty, none of us would have foreseen
the leader of our most feared gang one day becoming the Mayor of the
Borough!
Sharing a close friendship with Fred Rees inevitably led me to note the
attractions of his two elder sisters; Dorothea, the younger of the two had
in the year 1932 run full tilt into a lamppost whilst playing some game or
other. She apparently knocked herself unconscious and caused quite a
stir amongst the neighbours. Fred was vociferate in his description of the
catastrophe and along with 'half the avenue' I went along to see the
young lass. Young to me she was then, being three years my junior. In
all events, she had little to show for the experience apart from a lump the
size of a cricket ball across her forehead. Even the one projecting tooth
that I found in later years to be an infinite attraction, had failed to become
dislodged. I mention this in passing because the same skinny bundle of
impishness would one day be sliding my wedding ring onto her finger.
Grappling with the problems of wireless assembly was now fading into
virtual obscurity, as radio sets, ready made to merely plug into the
electricity supply flooded the shops. Father now looked to other
pursuits. It would be the camera and the telescope, both objects of deep
interest in the mind of any compulsive self assembly fanatic; and there
were plenty about at that time. Cameras that took the shelves of the
average shop would be of the 'box' variety and though quite effective
would have little in comparison to the plate camera and the enlargers of

the professional. That's where the 'Exchange and Mart' came in. Lenses and condensers, bromide paper and rolls of film soon flooded through the post, and decidedly mother was in for a hectic time. The area under the stairs was commandeered for a 'dark room' where an enlarger would be built to crown the whole process of 'home photography' and upstairs a new flight of stairs was to be installed to give access to the attic, where a telescope, big enough to attract half the population of Waterfoot would eventually poke its spellbinding apex to a distant star. We always knew where to find Dad; when he was on the night shift, he would pass his spare time under the stairs, and when he was on the day shift, he would spend it up in the attic. The telescope though, for some unknown reason died a mysterious death. It was built from cardboard tubes which Uncle Jack acquired from the paper mill in Ramsbottom, and I suspect that one night, prior to a heavy storm the awe inspiring wonder had inadvertently been left thrust to the sky, and disintegrated in the consequent deluge. So we heard little of its sad demise.

Not so the photographic venture. That went ahead in leaps and bounds. Roll film replaced the glass plate as shutters became faster and faster. There seemed no need now to sit for what seemed an eternity holding a false smile whilst the seconds ticked by for a time exposure; and now with a compressed air attachment, it was possible for Dad to dash on to the picture himself, after setting up his tripod. He made it altogether a lucrative sideline, with many of the neighbours calling on his talents; though he eventually lost all he had gained when voluntary schemes took heavy toll in war time.

Essential as it had become to have some form of sweeper, now we all appeared to be enjoying the luxury of at least ONE carpet, the Ewbank was normally the accepted extravagance. But not so now the infamous 'Hoover Man' was making his debut among the working classes. It was the birth of the dreaded double N; 'never, never'. Along our avenue, and from behind many a door, eyes would scan the road to see which threshold he crossed. Who would be next to part with half a crown a week and own this symbol to a new age of drudgery free living? As must be noted, we were living in a period of great depression, an economic slump of a magnitude not since experienced. And Dad in his deep wisdom forecast a bleak picture of impending capitalist doom should the 'On the Knocker' system ever take root. It was, he said, to be avoided like the plague; if people wanted this new fangled American carpet sweeper with a motor in it, then they should save up and buy it when they had sufficient cash. Needless to say, mother had to wait, and in the meantime we leaned on the broom, casting a mean eye at the 'Hoover Man' as he threaded his way, shouldering that evil token, from door to door. Fathers words may yet ring true, as sixty years later the distribution of easy credit still gathers momentum; where is the bursting point? We sat back to listen snuggly to John Snagge read the news, Christopher Stone play the records, and Paul Temple sort out the 'baddies' on a smart new radio that had been paid for!

For a long period in the early twenties, father must certainly have been saving very hard. He announced one day we were to have a holiday in the Irish Republic, then a comparatively new state, known better then as 'The Irish Free State'. Many men from this once British colony had fought alongside our own troops during the Great War and one of them, known to us a Uncle Paddy, had been a great friend of his. This was who we were going to visit, and although father had concessions on the railway owned ship, to afford a cabin was out of the question.

So in conformity with hundreds of others, we settled down onto seats strewn with portmanteaus, suitcases and trunks to have just about the most devastating sea crossing I can ever recall. My memory recaptures nothing but green seas, howling winds and torrential rain; it seemed to spread with rapture into every nook and cranny of an equally green deck. As if the emerald isle was intent upon promoting an ethnic tinge long before we even steadied a quaking foot on its thankful land. Of the holiday, I recall the landing, though little else, apart from the perpetual vomiting, and then putting foot in the depths of old Ireland and being able to understand not a word of their colourful English. It would be twenty years before the Irish Sea tempted me into another crossing, and thankfully by then, the ships that plied those turbulent waters had undergone substantial improvements. Surprisingly the experience, far from dampening a desire to travel, increased it even further.

Essentially there was full happiness in my childhood; illnesses which perhaps I took more than a fair share of, came and went, they were I presumed a necessary progression to normal living. If there was fun to be had, I was never far away, and if there wasn't, then I made it.

Those were my recollections as I sat that day, awaiting the major one that would see me fill a school bag for the very last time. Only two sad occasions I recalled of those early years. At six years of age, I had witnessed our dog run over by a car; one of the infrequent ones ever to pass the door and he had died in my arms. The trauma of that little event hurt for many months, and was followed in quick succession by my father succumbing to the rigours of trench warfare over a period of four devastating years. Despite the passing of ten years, the lingering mental scars were rampant in the men of his time. He was taken away to hospital suffering from a nervous breakdown and delayed shellshock and later to a convalescent home in Cornwall. For mother to travel with me and my baby brother a distance like that to visit him, was unthinkable. In today's reckoning it was the equivalent of setting out on a journey to the south of Europe, and consequently we saw nothing of our dad for many a month. The only two poignant events that marred and otherwise happy childhood.

CHAPTER 4

SCOUTING BOOTS

The charming village of Wray, lying to the north west of the Bowland
Forest, and deep in the shadow of Tatam and Salter Fells was the scene
of 'Hopkins Own' scout camp for the summer of 1936. Our venue was
a field alongside the River Hyndburn and wonderfully situated a little to
the north of Hornby where the river joins its big brother, the Lune. The
approach to Wray had been a little piece of heaven. Rumbling along in
Ridhalgh's old lorry we viewed scenery far beyond our expectations.
Against a brilliant blue skyline rose the unmistakable contours of
Ingleborough, and beyond Silverdale, the shadowy outline of the
Cumbrian mountains. Before we ever arrived, I knew this country was
for me. Our last camp had been at Golborne, skirting industrial Lancashire and a wonderful experience; yet who could compare the surround-
ings; here was a pure air. Breezes that were scented with the heathers
and wild flowers, unlike the polluted smog that choked the environs of
Wigan and Warrington.
Thirty seven scouts, a record number were to attend this camp. Those
who could not be accommodated on the ever faithful lorry came by cycle
or by train. Some names I recall were Sam Holt, Jim Ashworth, Herbert
Meex, 'Bullman', Bob Teasdale, Roland Jackson, Jack Stott and Bert
Dyer. In my own age group there was Fred Rees, David Whittaker,
Geoffrey Colbert, Tom Wheelan, Joe White, Cecil Ogden, Keith Brennan,
Jackson Holt and Jim Cross; then there were the Whitbread brothers,
Roy, Albert and Norman, and of course, the Scout Master, Norman
Jackson.
The entire concept of scouting was exemplified at this, the most
memorable mass camp that came my way. In ensuing years my
preference became the smaller, and more intimate gathering, even to the
extent of lone camping. But at this, comradeship, the pure exhilaration
of clean living, and a wealth of ingenuity went into welding a near perfect
little community. It staggered the local villagers who eyed proceedings
with an ever increasing amazement. In a matter of a few days a
suspension bridge, built entirely of logs and a mass of rope spanned a
forty foot neck of the river and provided a short cut to the village. Then

from apparently nowhere appeared rustic tables, seats, wash stands, towel rails and a host of other gadgets. The whole enterprise evoked the spirit of true pioneering, the very aim in the teachings of Baden Powell. When the 'day off' came along, that was the day we all went berserk and squandered the bulk of our spending money, the majority of the lads chose to go off to the seaside at Morecambe. In preference my own inclinations took me to Bentham, a considerable walk along the highway, but I had a passion at the back of my mind, and that was to learn to play the mouth organ; here now was my chance. In a shop here they relieved me of the grand total of one shilling, my entire savings, and in return I walked out the proud possessor of a Honer 'De Luxe', a constant companion for some considerable time. The journey back was much quicker, I think I walked twice as fast in a desperation to try my luck. And luck I had. Perhaps I had an 'ear' for it, as the saying goes. Back on the site, where only the assistant scout master remained in charge I headed for our patrols camp fire, threw a few sticks onto the low embers and out of earshot set about mastering this little one shilling orchestra. By the time all were back from their travels, I was knocking out 'When I grow too old to dream'. a popular ballad of the day, and round the camp fire that evening I had transgressed to a far higher plain in the appreciative estimation of my 'buddies'.

That harmonica was the first in a succession, and gave immeasurable pleasure to a host of youngsters and adults alike. You could say it was as much the portable entertainment of yesterday, as the transistor radio is of today, and only Adolf Hitler was responsible for cutting my supply line in the early forties.

In truth, it was this particular camp that sealed my devotion to outdoor pursuits. I knew it could never be any different; the smell of the wood smoke, the call of the night owl or the moorland curlews and the peewits. Camp fire cooking and the sing-song around dying embers at night, or to watch an eerie moon climb steadily high, through a backcloth of a starkly silhouetted pine. It was to become a dedication.

In time, my thoughts would inevitably turn to lone camping. It is because by nature, I am a loner. Reading a feature in the 'Scout' of July 1937, I still have it, the inspiration burned deep. It opens with the words by Rudyard Kipling. "Who hath smelt wood-smoke at twilight? Who hath heard the birch log burning? Who is quick to read the noises of the night?" These words, and those that followed captured the very soul of this susceptible reader. It was decisive.

Now I was leaving school. A job had been secured and my little world was changing. Two years ago we had left the windswept confines of Edgside and the little pleasures that seemed so great at the time were now a nonentity. Behind me now, but crystal clear; dashes up to Whittakers for a pennyworth of gobstoppers, the tin roofed dug outs on the waste ground across from the house, and the treasured walks over the Hile to Bacup 'Rec', and the 'boat swings'. Annual pantomimes at Bethesda Chapel and haymaking in the summer at Able Heaps where we helped out the Irishmen who came for the season. There had been trips on the train to Hollingworth Lake, the excitement of the big freeze up in the early thirties and the heat wave that followed after the spring, we all queued up in a long winding line to fill buckets from a spring along the top road. Straw palliasses for those that were really hard up, and flock mattresses for the many, feather for the wealthy. No longer would I be grabbing Betty Dunbar of Dorothy Hodgkinson as they ran through the 'ginnel' at Mill End.

Nor would we revel in the opportunity to chance our luck with the girls, as the lights dimmed for the 'Lantern Lectures' in Piercy Church. Baggy, knee length shorts, that drew every blast of an Arctic wind around your vitals had been cast and replaced by equally baggy long grey trousers at the acceptable age of 13 and now we were feeling truly adult.

And as school days drew to a close there was one regret I harboured closely. For a succession of years my school holidays had allowed a week's stay with cousins in Ramsbottom. There were 'naughty' parties and fun galore around Crow Lane, but what I would miss dearly were the visits to the railway station where endless hours were spent watching the signalman at work from the footbridge steps. These nostalgic memories I have penned in a book 'Railway Lines and Levers' and it would be pointless to repeat them here. That pastime, and the proximity of the railway to the house we moved into on leaving Edgside were to have a strong influence on my future working career.

To think that we had moved into the Station Master's house, one would have expected a little pointed affluence about the building, but lo and behold, we were back to gas lights and an outside toilet. An imposingly large place with a huge garden but as became all railway property at that time, a sad lack of modernisation. It was all great fun to we youngsters however; something different, and what greater than the railway running by only ten feet from the front door!

Again, there were new friends to make, though in retrospect there was but one true one. One that was worth a dozen of some of the acquaintances that cross life's path, and the type that would share you his last 'fag' willingly if you were without. Whereas my eldest son was to be named after Fred Rees, my second took the name of this ever congenial chum, Douglas Taylor.

Douglas had an Alsatian dog, 'Snip' and had it not been for the war the two would have been inseparable. Within a very short time, Doug and Snip became integral to our happy band of wanderers, and signalled the start to a long sequence of unforgettable experiences.

Hardly had we settled into our fresh surroundings when there was great excitement. Hills pickle works at the bottom of Greenbridge was ablaze, and it was only across Rough Lee woods from the top of our garden. My little sister was only twelve months old, and even she got dragged across to the vantage point overlooking the conflagration. There were dozens of jars exploding in the intense heat and all sounded like a battlefield in the melee below us. In the aftermath however, little salvage came to light for inveterate scavengers such as us. Not like the substantial pickings we had when the rubber works burnt down at the bottom of Shawclough Road in Scout Bottom. Here there had been rubber soles and heels for a countless supply of shoes all flung clear of the inferno, and enough to shod the feet of the entire population of Edgside and Whitewell Bottom for the next decade. And didn't we have a free 'pop' when staff at Bowness's next door heaped crates galore out on the roadside to escape the risk of explosion. What a party. And all for free!

Between times young Dorothea Rees would come around to take out my baby sister in the new 'marmet' pram. I had little eyes for Dorothea at that time, but the pram she was pushing I thought could have been turned into a superb trolley at one time.

And then the big day arrived. The hollow ring of a hundred feet pounding the imposing stairways of Lea Bank school were past. The ultimate school reference I had collected was a further inference to my potential and that I really felt somewhat unaccountable, as I still felt the strings of 'Pa' Turner's slipper across the buttocks.

Now the wide world awaited. I found myself apprenticed in the boot and shoe engineering trade with a job that subsequently failed to hold any attraction. A stable career seemed to be far from my mind anyway at that

time, but it was employment, and the world was wide open. I counted
myself lucky with a wage of five shillings (25 pence) and weekly pocket
money of one shilling (five pence). After all, a quarter of the population
had no work at all, and a multitude of youngsters leaving school were
immediately tagged on to the end of a long dole queue.

Possessing all the failings of the average youngster, and not long after
picking up file, hacksaw and oil can, the dubious attraction of the nicotine
weed showed its ugly head. My two fellow mechanics sucked lustily at
the burning capillary and coughed heartily back in appreciation. It was
all so manly, I considered, and joined them.

Predictably, it became the cause of eternal pennylessness. An ability to
pose as an assumed man of the world, countered by an inability to jangle
a few coins in one's pocket.

A packet of five Woodbines, Park Drive or Star would relieve you of two
pence, or the machine outside Sam Howarths, one penny, and that for
a slim packet of two Churchmans' Number One Specials! With a grand
total of a mere twelve pence for the week's divertisements there was little
left for other pleasures, apart from the few one generated by pure
inventiveness. That is why the habit of 'docking' a cigarette was
customary, it was instinct to nip the fag after a given number of gasps, and
there was no need to count. At exactly half way down the weed would
be extinguished to spend the next one hour in the dark seclusion of a top
left pocket in the boiler suit.

Along with the aid of a tuppenny 'Rizla' hand machine huge economies
could be made; your older and more affluent workmates may well have
thrown and extra large 'dog end' on the floor and these, aided by the
addition of a few dried tea leaves could produce a splendid spate of ear
shattering expectorations. In retrospect it was vile, and probably in the
light of present day thinking would come as a surprise to realise that as
each Christmas came round our Xmas 'box' would more than likely be
an attractive cellophaned box of fifty 'Passing Cloud' or 'Piccadilly'. An
acceptable present from your parents could weil be a glittering chrome
plated cigarette case with 'knicker elastic' stretching across the two sides
to hold the hopeful quantity of twenty of these cancer sticks. We were
a society highly unconscious of medical repercussion. As today, there
were beckoning temptations; the photo cigarette cards issued by 'Senior
Service' a new brand now circulating were fabulous. Their price, at ten
for sixpence was beyond my pocket but I struggled hard and cadged

well the series 'Beautiful Britain' and a particular attraction 'Railways of Britain'. They left all other cigarette cards of the period well behind, and offered a superb collection.

Taking into account my lack of enthusiasm for all that spelled monotony, breaks from the boring task of filing endless steel fittings for stapling machines, tempering in hot oil and the ice cold water, the task of cleaning the boss's car was more than welcome. Out of Mr. Ralph's sight and in the open air it was possible to eke out a wily hour polishing his Morris '8' to perfection. I note he never allowed me to clean the inside of it, or to open the sides of the bonnet to see how it all worked. Presumably he had already noted a total absence of any mechanical brilliance. But Mr. Grieg the foreman, allowed me to use both the telephone and the typewriter in HIS absence. That was more in my line. Telephones were not an appliance every fourteen year old lad was in the habit of using. Extemely few houses would possess such a luxury and I thrilled no end when first taking the receiver off the rest. I was expected for those precious minutes to take down orders from various slipper mills and then type out information onto the order sheets.

Behind the din of lathes, milling machines and electric drills though, I was to learn quickly the one thing I dreaded, and that was how to use my fists. As a timid lad, I shuddered when it came to a potential scrap, but when unexpectedly provoked could even surprise myself. It seemed I was bequeathed quite a little 'paddy' under that shock of red hair I carried. It first manifested after undue provocation and ended in a pool of blood from my adversaries broken nose. It was a grim forecast of several fights that would shadow the path of a boy climbing from adolescence to maturity.

They would come all in good time. For now, it was the call of the local moors that beckoned.

Waugh's Well, a stone memorial built around the spring that bucked the turf of the upper Turn Valley was ever a focal point. And Fo' Edge Farm, sadly demolished for unknown reasons by the Water Board in more recent years, was where as kids, we had our tea and sandwiches. The well was first built in 1866 some twenty four years before Edwin Waugh the celebrated Lancashire dialect poet died, and then at the height of his fame. Stone for the project was donated by Lord Crawshaw, quarry owner, then Thomas Brooks of Crawshawbooth. In 1966, when found to be in a sad state of decline, it was rebuilt by dedicated enthusiasts and a stone inscription to the well known naturalist and rambler Ward Ogden, in HIS memory added.

From this point the paths, mostly of our own making, led to streams and dells of infinite appeal; at least to we of the self titled 'Dawn Patrol'. These admirable locations provided a variety of encampments which we were to frequent for the forthcoming decade and found themselves honoured with such evocative titles as 'Windy Creek', 'Red River Valley', 'Smoky Canyon', 'Primus Gulch and 'Fern Creek' amongst others. The latter I think found the greatest favour and saw the smoke of our camp fire the most often.

It came about, there is little doubt, from the early association Fred Rees and myself had with the likes of Ward Ogden, the Pennine Paths society and of that of the I.L.P. ramblers group.

These were the hills most frequented and where our roots were buried, and when given our first freedom to go it alone, the Rooley Moors were the first to beckon. Had a modern day backpacker witnessed our departure he would likely have had an attack of palpitation, as from the rear both Fred and I were virtually invisible; only the lower half of four legs appeared to be suspending the enormous packs consisting of tents, ground sheets, sleeping bags, billie cans, half a dozen loaves, enamel pots and plates and amongst other miscellaneous necessities, a half dozen tins of baked beans.

On this occasion, the pair of us left, and we were given blessings by both of our parents. They were sure we had had sufficient training in the rudiments of self survival, and they were right. No shops, no other humans, no man made comforts would be encountered on these bleak uplands; only curlews and peewits, the wind, and an eerie silence that could penetrate the very soul; but they forgot the rain. And rain it did. We had left in brilliant sunshine, and a light that brings the hills to within touching distance; abnormally pristine. A clarity laced with distrust. Two hours later the sky was black and the heavens opened; and stayed open for the four days we persevered in claiming acceptance to the mythical realms of British pigheadedness. When our two respective fathers appeared through the curtain of dense moorland cloud they were relieved and not a little surprised. They had set out on a mission of rescue and not expected to find the little scene of total self sufficiency that we had established in the past four days. From the discarded stone, wood and other debris that surrounded the site of a disused mine, the makings of a rainproof fire, oven spit roasting device were readily available, and we had put it all to good use. Accumulated at one side was firewood to last many a day, and drinking water was available in quantity from several nearby streams. In all, a scene of complete tranquility and orderliness, not what they had expected.

The inclement weather had done nothing to dampen our ardour; on the contrary, it had been a challenge and we knew we had experienced almost the worst. The visual beauty of these moors was in the eyes of the beholder, and this we had.

With this given enthusiasm the two of us kindled a strong unity within our little band of seven. To plan our weekend camps and any other escapades we set about finding a suitable little headquarters and eventually this came about in the form of a disused hen cote which the farmer above Rough Lea leased to us for a shilling a week. It stunk to high heaven but with fourteen willing hands to scrape out the dung, and the aid of a couple of bottles of disinfectant, donated by some unaware parent, it became a temple of teenage independence. We even had a password to gain admittance; you knocked on the door with a pre-arranged code and the one inside would call, ''The rangers must survive''; then you answered with the affirmative ''They'r bound to'', and the door was opened. Never did anyone fail to give the appropriate answers because I don't think anyone else knew of our existence! And where necessary dialogue arose I fail to recall; in probability it had been read in some 'Zane Grey', or heard spoken in some 'Bill Boyd' western of the time. 'Westerns' were, and hopefully will remain, a strong influence on the pioneering instincts of adventurous youth. In evidence that is where such names as 'Fern Creek' arose.

Masses of these fronds swept down from the lower slopes of Knowle Hill and into this valley we gave a name. The stream stumbled from the adjacent peat bogs of Scout Moor, and it was alongside these infatuating banks we pitched our tents so often. Winter or summer, spring or autumn, it mattered little. In the summer our ever faithful companion 'Snip' would catch us a rabbit, in the winter he would act as our foot warmer in a curled up ball at the foot of the tent. Well do I remember the day he showed canine reluctance to this form of relegation. It had been an unusually quiet night for the month of January. Deadly serene and what we considered unseasonably warm. When daylight cracked and Dougy stretched from his sleeping bag to untie the cords of the tent flap, we found out why. In cascaded a four foot avalanche of crisp virgin snow, and across the back of our comrade Snip; at that he took offence. Up he shot into the middle of the tent, arched his back and showered the entire offering into the faces of the other three hitherto inert sleepers. I've never seen campers rise so quickly ever.

If not gracing the banks of this particular haven, our green canvas may well be spotted high on the windswept bluff of Turf Moor, among the course brown turf that succoured only ants and a sprinkling of moorland birds. Here the wind in the gulleys was keen, it carried rain from the western approaches to the slopes of the ever thirsty Pennines. Here too, was a moorland denied its rightful maturity by decades of industrial pollution, but we thought little of those controversies; this was our environment; our heritage. This small dell in the folds of rolling moor we had christened 'Windy Creek'.

All sites justified a strong reasoning behind their allotted titles. 'Smoky Canyon' was the small gulley in which we never succeeded in finding an appropriate position to establish the camp fire. Whatever the way the wind was blowing, it never failed to coil a plume of dense smoke, and send it lovingly into one or other of the tents, and however much we all appreciated the smell of green wood burning, the choking fumes from an assortment of gorse and any other combustible debris that could be scavenged on those wastes, was considered obnoxious. But the love of a camp fire, and all its intrinsic signification was bred deep. The primus stove, humped for many a mile, and on many an occasion was virtually a non starter. It was looked down upon as a totally degrading object, to be put to use only in the direst of circumstances. At 'Primus Gulch', aptly named after those conditions were met, it rose up from the bowels of my rucksack to greet a world of near Arctic severity. There were two hardy individuals present only, Fred Rees and myself, I now forgive the rest who deserted the faithful, for the weather was diabolical. The stream, at this point, normally the very essence of cascading tranquility had stopped dead. It was frozen completely, as if a wand had been raised and stopped the flow in one miraculous split second. A scene of wondrous delight to the one with paint and canvas; to us a sight of unbridled self pity. You see, we would persist in acting the little 'tough guys', and shivering uncontrollably in knee length scout shorts.

At least the paraffin and meths did not freeze. After a fruitless search for something burnable, the half hearted attempt was abandoned, and we

got to work with numbed fingers on our new found friend the Primus. It
worked like a dream and I must confess, I've never been so glad to see
that little spurt of blue flame. A handful or two of gleaming crisp icicles
from the nearest waterfall into the dixie and five minutes later a steaming
mug of welcome tea. And what of undressing that night and putting on
pyjamas; well the pyjamas went on, but only on top of everything else
there was to wear. Then the boots came off, and went quickly on again,
as did the balaclava mother had recently knitted. I had hinted at looking
a cissy wearing that, but wear it I did that night, as no-one would ever
see me two feet down from the pillow. For exercise at daybreak, we
kicked each other into life, then tossed up for who would go outside the
tent and repeat the novelty of breaking further ice from the solid stream,
or who would have the tempting pleasure of lighting up the stove to melt
the frozen breath that gripped the canvas walls.
Predictably the weekend finished as they all did; on the last few miles to
home, tentative plans were being made for next week's venture.
Of the regulars that pitched their tents on these moors at the time, apart
from myself, Fred Rees, Douglas Taylor, David Whittaker, Jim Cross,
Tom Wheelan, Geoffrey Colbert and Bill Suffle, I fail to recall who had
the brilliant idea of placing a moderate sized piece of cake under a stone
to keep an otherwise troublesome army of ants at bay. It happened on
the night we were late arriving in 'Red River Valley' a site below Waughs
Well that gained its name. I know not how. Probably we had recently
seen Gene Autry in the film of that name. However, here we were, tent
pitched and ground sheet spread. Rolled up newspapers filling gaps in the
uneven tufts. Outside it was an evil night, black and laced in moorland fog.
The night you snuffed the candle early and slid down into the welcome
depths of a cosy sleeping bag. And that we did. Only then, perhaps five
minutes later, was it revealed someone had a malicious stone, pointed
and uncompromising, sticking into his ribs. That should have proved little
worry as the besieged wrestled with the stone under his ground sheet,
but the moment he succeeded in dislodging the perpetrator, was when
the fun all started. There was total chaos now as what could surely have
been a million highly indignant ants swarmed across one and all. It was
mayhem as sleeping bags, rucksacks and anything to hand flew in all
directions. Then it was that our saviour played his master stroke. Diving
out from under the tent flap and into the grub tent, he made a rapid forage
and returned with a huge chunk of appetising fruit cake. This he placed

with practised hands into the gaping hole, and, as if by a wave of a wand, the million disoriented ants returned in military precision to attack the bait. On top went the stone again, and over that a heap of handy newspapers. The tent could be re-pitched on the morrow. That night we slept well.

Our enterprising sorties, in effect an activity unofficial, yet quite within the scouting spirit had come to the ears of Norman Jackson, our Scout Master. Apparently impressed, he was in need of someone to take charge of a group of young cubs who were to be initiated into the joys of camping at Holmes Chapel, some five or six miles away in the Cliviger Valley. Although the eldest of us was little over the age of fifteen, he delegated responsibility to three of us, Geoffrey Colbert, Fred Rees and myself. We felt ourselves highly honoured and would take up the task with all seriousness. At first all appeared easy going; but we underestimated the demoralising impact of fifteen rowdy eight to ten year olds. It all started well at the Scout Room where the two treck carts were loaded high with tents, kit bags and all the paraphernalia needed for a four day camp. Despite their boisterous flinging of equipment, which invariably went clean over the top and landed on someone's head at the other side, the job was completed in good time, and all roped together. At that point, it is all hands to the shafts and to the ropes which hang from the cart side to aid in either pulling forwards uphill or backwards downhill as the case may be. And away we set to trudge the long climb from Lumb to Toll Bar and down the long descent to Townley; and, to take an unexpected yet unforgettable lesson in child psychology.

Incredulous as it sounds, or at least it did to us at that immature age, when only a mile had been covered and as the first steep section of the route loomed ahead, one little mite complained heartily of a blister on his foot. Feeling compassionate we hoisted him on top of the cart to rest and view proceedings from his vantage point, and the amazing fact was that as the road steepened and the load appeared to become heavier, another, and yet another of these wily souls developed imaginary blisters on the feet, or sore hands from ropes they pulled on. Consequently, at the summit, and about to start the tortuous descent there were two carts piled to overflowing, a crew of half the pack of cubs balanced precariously on bulging kit bags, and only half the allotted hands to control this potential runaway. And runaway it all but did. Passing the notorious 'brick works bend' the faith put into us by our elders all but melted into oblivion as we

ground the steel banded wheels into the kerbside.
The ropes dangled free with no-one to take the strain, and still both carts were gaining momentum. Now it became desperate as the last, but most difficult hair pin danced towards us and our racing legs were turning to jelly. There was only one way to finish the fiasco; the wheels ground painfully along the kerbstones, the trucks bucked and rolled; sparks streamed from the hot steel bands and the loads tilted to impossible angles. Scout poles broke like matchsticks in a last attempt to sprig the wheels, but it worked. Half way into that final bend, we stopped; finally..............with a shattering jolt.

There seemed no trace now of blisters or any other ailment as the subdued pack dropped quickly to the ground, only one was missing and we found him huddled deep in the morass of equipment and safely cocooned in a sheath of blankets. Significantly, they now were intent on helping all they could, and quite prepared to walk every inch of the way. It had been a traumatic ten minutes but ended in laughter and a nonchalant shrug of the shoulders. The episode passed, the rest of the Whitsuntide break was a resounding success and we returned home to receive accolades from the troops elders and amass a few more points towards another badge.

CHAPTER 5

DIRTY BOOTS

Badges were not my strong point, I had achieved the cookery and first aid token but specialisation in a given subject is hardly my aspiration. My nature is that of a Jack of all Trades. Nevertheless, had badges or stripes been forthcoming in the field of musical interest, then one may well have come my way.

My father's own interest, his collection of classical records and later my efforts on the harmonica had nurtured a keen appreciation, particularly in the melodic or lively sections of the popular classics.

To sit then in respectful awe as Mr. Taylor, Douglas's father, swept through the closing passages of 'Poet and Peasant' and 'William Tell' on the piano keyboard was an hour spent in sheer bliss. It so happened that Mr. Taylor had been, up to the present time, a pianist employed by cinemas screening the silent movies. Now their day was coming to a close, but a musician must play on. For a decade, he had sat offside the screen to accompany the film; find the right mood music to suit the scene. A furious burst from William Tell as horsemen dash across the screen, or a poignant few bars from Romeo and Juliet as Rudolf Valentino embraces the glamorous Mary Pickford. The wizardry of his flying fingers were followed by at least a half dozen of us during his practice hours in the parlour room of their home in Ivy Street. Huddled up on the sofa and religiously quiet, as we were expected to be, his playing was spellbinding, and from those early times, I have been hooked on the likes of Beethoven, Mozart and Rossini.

And away from the strains of these classical composers, or even the likes of jazz and boogie, I was an avid reader. Not only of railway literature, which had become a minor passion and would determine my future, but to the novels of the Brontes and the lighter scan of youthful magazines. Favourites of mine were 'Boys Cinema' and 'The Scout'.

Of a great significance was an article I read in the latter magazine in the year 1937. Great enthusiasm was penned to the wonders of cycle touring, and around the same time I had caught sight of Fred's elder sister, Gladys, hurtling along Bacup Road on her new 'Parlite', then to meet up with the Rossendale Wheelers. It all set me thinking, and I

approached Dad. Yes, it was all possible now I was bringing in a wage,
the first thing would be to save some of that spending money, instead of
squandering it on fags and the 'pictures'.
So it came about in two or three weeks, I was leaning a 28" wheeled ex
post office bike against a lamp post and learning the wonders of
propelling myself along on two wheels. That was if I wasn't falling off the
monster. There seemed an awful lot of dried blood along the rutted back
streets behind the 'Duke of Buccleuch'. The bike had been far too large
for me but the art was learned and the enthusiasm was noted. It had been
ten shillings well spent. In less than a month, a brand new Raleigh sports
model graced the ostentatiously titled 'hallway' at railway cottages. It
would be the first, and very last NEW machine I would ever go astride
for the next ten years; despite riding the entire length and breadth of Great
Britain.
Initially all went well. With four pounds, nineteen shillings and sixpence
in his pocket, father took me across to Greenwood and Parsons, the new
cycle shop that had recently opened at the front entrance to Waterfoot
Arcade. It is worth mentioning that this Victorian structure housed the
Billiard hall, a den of iniquity we teenagers were taught to shun. This was
where one mourned a misspent youth. Through the smoky haze we
glimpsed jacketless men contorting themselves into all sorts of weird
positions round the tables in an effort to pot a ball, and an all too evident
swanky display of watch chains across the buttoned waistcoats. On
occasions, by crafty positioning at the doorway a ha'penny could be
earned running down to Tommy Hartley's with a basin and bringing back
chips and a good helping of 'Tommy's' black peas. Sometimes, it was
a 'Holland's' meat pie soaked in this leguminous mass. Yes, we loved
our arcade, and now, the tantalising array of gleaming new bikes that
embellished its facade.
The Raleigh 'sports' model was the only one for me; I fell for the shape
of the handlebars! As an attractive a thought as that of a young lady's
thighs that would come before very long. In addition to a three speed hub
gear, it sported a Pifco dynamo lighting set, they cost seven shillings and
sixpence, and that, at the time was the total fine awarded you for either
riding without lights at night, or caught cycling along the pavement. The
next task would be to save hard for the pannier bags, the one-man ultra
lightweight tent, and cooking utensils necessary to put into effect the all
inspiring pastime the journalist had predicted..... With great relish I

started, then went and spoilt it all.

I suppose a reluctance to conform, to accept the advice of one's elders, and to behave rationally was the cause. I was growing up, or so I thought. Passing through the 'fella lad' period as the locals called it. Could it have been the Hollywood influence? I did a lot of silly things in that next twelve months; smoked too much, which ruined any chance of purchasing the things I had promised myself, strutted around in the best imitations of Cagney and Bogart. Trilby at the appropriate angle, and a cigarette hanging from the corner of the mouth, and mimicking the stance of the great Edward G. Robinson or George Raft. But worse was to come.

An orgy of teenage lust was the subsequent first phase. Maturity had showed its ugly head and perhaps my libido was in some way excessive. Whatever the cause, a succession of amorous adventures put me soon into conflict with father. First there were the wanton attentions of the girl from Newchurch. She threw everything at me including her craving virginity. The 'mill end' terror from the bottom of Turnpike who could make the eyes of two of us pop on the back row of the 'Kings'; and both at once. But it was the two licentious sisters in a now demolished farmhouse on the slopes of Higher Lench that were to cause the ultimate clash between father and son. They, along with an equally promiscuous cousin who made up a nymphomanical trio, were my downfall. In a succession of escapades the first was a sample of what was to come. In a freshly mown field alongside the farm father caught the pack of us in wild abandon enjoying life's oldest sport. What made it worse was the fact that my case of maths and English papers, was perched high on a sheaf of hay advertising my whereabouts to one and all, and at a time when I should have been studiously seated behind a desk at Alder Grange School taking evening classes!

In the end, we had a blazing row. Mother considered, in her wisdom, it was six of one, and half a dozen of the other. In those days, little was spoken of the dangers and consequences of licentious behaviour and in retrospect, that could have been the source of the friction that manifested. Whatever the reason, at that age, one has little thought for the psychology of teenage evolution. Nothing went right for the next week. There was a huge water rat that all but sank its teeth into my neck after cornering it in the workshop and flinging an axe at it. The day following my mop of red hair was sucked into the shaft drive of a powerful electric drill and that incident came close to scalping me. Finally, I lost a ten shilling note on my way to the post office to buy the firm's weekly 'Lloyd George' stamps, and that was double my week's wage. In truth, I was not happy.

In desperation now, and sick with self pity, I took the course of the boyhood heroes of the silver screen. Jackie Cooper had done it, so why not me. I ran away from home.

Ran away, would perhaps be a misinterpretation of the hackneyed phrase. In point of fact, I cycled away, taking the virtually new bike and riding off to seek fame and fortune in the Royal Navy; at Hull!

To anyone who is ignorant of the fact, Hull was a large fishing port, not a naval harbour. I was ignorant. To the east it lay, and was on the North Sea, and that was all I cared, as into the saddle I swung. There were various misadventures which culminated with an about turn somewhere on the banks of the Humber; sleeping the night wrapped in a cycle cape amidst the confines of a telephone box in Otley, and getting lost somewhere in the Yorkshire Dales, the following day. One meal only I had during the entire enterprise and then arrived home two days later with my tail between my legs, yet hopefully a little wiser.

A comfortable bed and food in my belly was all that passed of interest over the next few days; until I read a few lines of mortification in the classified advertisements of the Rossendale Free Press,..... there it was; 'Cycle for Sale, as new'.

I was stricken. It was all my own fault. The bike went, and slowly I returned to a more sanely lifestyle.

In the midsummer came the annual scout camp once more. Enthusiasm had not diminished despite these recent relapses into unruly behaviour, in fact I believe them to have taught me a few rudiments in the painful process of juvenile pre maturity.

The chosen site this year was at Caton. A stone's throw only from the point where Turner painted his famous landscape, 'The Crook of The Lune'. Idyllic and tranquil in the pastoral setting of Lonsdale, yet a mere five miles to the historic city of Lancaster.

The notes in my battered log book state, 'weather fair, a very enjoyable week'. It was a typical understatement. Vivid incidents come to mind; like the daunting challenge of two whole bucketful of potatoes waiting to be peeled. I'd never seen a 'Lancashire' potato peeler before, but saw plenty of it over the next few hours when detailed to take up the chore.

I found a lifetime's friend; at threepence in Woolworths 'threepenny and sixpenny store', they were unbeatable value. Even mother was presented one for her next birthday! We had surprises galore. Eels from the river which we were taught how to fry, 'sliced' bread which we had never seen before, that invention had yet failed to reach the remoter parts of Lancashire; on Parents Day they were all treated to 'green' tea, an anomaly we assured them was due to reflection of the green canvas tents! In effect, I understand polishing the inside of the dixie with a handful of virgin grass, before water and the 'Lipmans' was a added, created the illusion!

Amongst the parents and families that came along that week, mostly by train, there was an exception. It was Gladys, Fred's elder sister, and she had cycled here, all of fifty miles each way and the occurrence would not be forgotten. One day I swore to be back in the saddle. Despite a hammering I had taken on the road to Hull, the seed had been sown.

Perhaps the day to be noted, or to be in preference deemed a day of notoriety, in this week of youthful exuberance was when a nameless bespectacled youth in our patrol found his larger than average 'masculinity' trapped securely in a milk bottle! I may point out the milk bottle of our time had an extra large neck. He himself was prone to a little pride in his valued possession whilst several others were possibly overtaken by jealousy. We often remarked that due to his shortsightedness, one day he would trip over it. Which is what he almost did until two of the lads, eager to reduce his ego slipped the dreaded bottle over the end. But then the consternation set in. Far from the fun expected in defeating his challenge to the impossibility of achieving that deed, was the sight of his rapidly swelling member firmly ensconced in a non expandable piece of dreaded glass. We should have known better, but there again, there were no biology classes in our schools then. His resplendent symbol of elongated wedding equipment took a course that nature alone has decreed. It delved further down into the bottle and at the same time dug deep into the neck, slowly turning to a frightening spectrum of deep purple and bright pink. Stood there in the middle of the tent with 'Richard' at full attention, and an advertisement for the Co-op dairies perched on the end would hardly have been a suitable vista for the scout master should he pay a surprise visit at any moment, let alone the dairy manager. In clandestine silence he was hustled from the tent, where two of the heftier of us lifted him by the armpits and literally 'dipped' him in the river. And that river was VERY cold. Half naked he was lowered down, and the shock did the rest. We didn't see the bottle again, but it was noted when our friend was finally deposited once more on dry land, the girth of his 'pride' had rapidly diminished, and its head hung limp in shame! Back from the annual camp, and a spate of weekend camping followed. It inevitably did, and Fern Creek as ever was a magnet. Predictably, some incident of note would arise, as it always did. This time it was Tom Wheelan and the infamous meat pie. 'Hollands' it was, but that point is immaterial; the fact was it contained meat, and Tom was a Roman Catholic, and the day concerned was a Friday.

There were eight of us on this occasion, five in the tent I occupied, and that included Tom. We all knew it was a Friday when we arrived but Tom had overlooked the significance in the current excitement. The pies had been a resounding success, fresh that very morning we set out, and warmed in a biscuit tin oven we devised over the camp fire; drowned in mushy peas who could ask for a more scrumptious treat in the mid evening. Dusk had descended and finally nightfall. We had our cocoa and slid through the tent flap and down into a cosy sleeping bag. The candle was snuffed and five heads lay to rest; hopefully.

Only in the twilight of subconsciousness, and during a haze of happy reflections did the awful impact strike him. He was distraught, he woke every one of us; what could he do, what was the answer? We told him to lie down and forget it. But no, he would have to atone. For the rest of the night and throughout the following day he worried; normally he was such a volatile lad, we felt he would surely have some sort of breakdown. Then at tea time someone had the most obvious answer: to confess!

That was all very well in theory, but no Roman Catholic priest was ever likely to be tramping these moors, and less still at this time of the day or even at night. But of course, if he cared to get up at five in the morning and tramp the five miles into Ramsbottom he may find a suitable church in which to confess his dastardly deed. It would be Sunday wouldn't it. We laughed; He didn't. That was brilliant idea; why hadn't he thought of it before. And so, with mind at rest and a good evening meal round the camp fire behind us we slid under the canvas about eleven o'clock. Even Snip curled up at the tent foot more speedily than normal, he himself considered all matters to have been amicably settled.

Of course he. not understanding the enigmas of human behaviour was totally wrong. Tom shot up from his sleeping bag, 'what about an alarm clock?' At five in the morning it would be pitch dark and he was unlikely to awake by normal means. In those less affluent days not one of us carried a pocket watch, let alone an alarm. It was suggested he set off there and then, but that brought no response. Two hours later and still no sleep a further proposal that he sit outside and watch for daybreak carried no weight. Another hour passed and the moon rose, yet we couldn't convince Tom that was daybreak and get him out!

Yet sleep will come in good time. It came to us at probably five minutes before the catastrophe. As if our friend had after all possessed an inbuilt timing mechanism, he bolted upright at presumably what must have been the appropriate time. The trouble was that whereas he had attained the height of five feet, four inches, the ridge pole of the tent reached a bare four feet. The fun started. The cane splintered, the dog panicked, down came both support poles and over went two billie cans of dried beans soaking in water. No-one had a torch, and a match to the candle was impossible. Five bodies and a demented 'Alsatian' fought for a way out of the ensuing melee and then a light showed from the adjoining tent. We had our bearings at least. Extricated before a complete surrender to asphyxia we then looked round for Tom; but Tom had disappeared completely. Gone we knew well in haste to confess his sin; we hoped he would seek forgiveness for this last one before he got back..... and all because someone had the bright idea of bringing along factory made meat pies to a camp site. This, was reparation.

The joy perceived in reaching an imaginary mature age of fifteen was all the more fulfilled when I was awarded a rise in my wage. It was substantial; a fifty per cent increase, up from five shillings to seven shillings and sixpence. Though I doubt I should have received it had I not asked; that seemed to be the norm.

Nonetheless, the job I found exasperatingly boring. Apart from the ritual of annually whitewashing the workshop walls in order to conform to factory acts, it was dreary work; filing and even more filing. Again I was eager for small adventures. There were further flutters with damsels who were reluctant to say 'No', and another escapade in the notorious house of iniquity on the hillside. That inevitably resulted in another tiff with father and I ran away again. This time the eruption took me less far. The moors above Cowpe were my bed, and a rock hard attache case my pillow. That was until the cold set in; then I crept back down the valley and ended a long miserable night curled up in our outside toilet at the bottom of the yard. At seven the house door opened and in I went. That there must be

other ways than flying off in a tantrum to ease the passage through
delinquency was now a calm consideration, and from then on matters
appeared to resolve themselves. All forgiven and the twelve month 'itch'
put behind.

That was our last year on the banks of the Lune at Caton. It seemed that
water would be our greatest enemy. At the end of the week we were
flooded out with it and had to abandon the site prematurely, whilst almost
every day it rained. On the odd occasion it was fine, it was frustratingly
cold; the river in particular. Running water always will attract boys, and
we were no exception. We had waited all week to try our hand at
swimming in a large pool that was to be found in the fast flowing shallows
across from the camp. At the given time six of us stood astride a boulder
viewing the speeding waters that little time ago had plunged from the
barren heights of the Howgills. Six youths, that only yesterday had
flowered to pubescence. They stood ready to jump, and the events that
followed were a classical display of symmetrical precision. In perfect
time they plunged in, and in equally perfect time just three seconds later,
they soared out; each bolt upright and clasping two hands together in
frantic support of a pair of anaesthetised testicles. We wondered what
full castration would bring in the way of excruciating pain, and when
David Whittaker returned to the water, bent low and brought up a
rounded pebble to display, one and all began to ponder. Had that really
happened?

Like all good things in life, there is an end, or at least a change, to which
the young find hard to accept. At first the announcement that Dad was
to be transferred to Bury, some ten miles south and close to the suburbs
of Manchester came as a shock. Would I lose touch with my chums, lads
I had known since long before school days. Probably not, there was
always the train and as a railway family we had subsidised fares. The
blunt fact at least allowed a further six weeks to aid in its digestion, and
then we were off. It was a temporary farewell to the valley, but a lifestyle
I would never see again.

It happened the move could not have been better timed. Now approaching sixteen and anxious for a change of employment, the environs
of Manchester gave a far wider scope. My thoughts were turning to the
railway and to be employed in an undertaking which generated such
profound interest must surely be my target. That is where I set my sights,
but there would be many months to wait before that happy day arrived.

In the meantime, work was there for he who searched. First it was in the day long slog of pedalling or pushing an overloaded grocer's bike, with a basket of provisions and the like threatening to overturn me on every sharp bend in the road, or across every wet tramline. From that job the attraction of more money took me into a hat factory brushing the pile of steam hot felt from seven thirty in the morning until half past five in the evening, and ultimately to the L.M.S. Railway where my career took off as a signal box lad. It was to be one of the happiest periods of my life and its consequences and times I have narrated in 'Railway Lines and Levers'.

For a short time the vicinity of Gig Lane, Bury's football club venue was our home, a little to the south of the town, and from there to Waterfoot, where my pals had been deserted, was in the region of ten miles. That was by road, field, footpath and moor; a little further by bus, tram or train. So with little money to spare after the infernal 'weeds' had taken too large a slice of any allowance, it was to terra firma I set my feet. On a Sunday, it was away to an early start and the call of the moors. On to visit the likes of Fred, Dougy and David, then the lonely tramp home cross hill and dale.

Serenely wonderful is the feel of the one who walks alone. It is the smell of the moors, the taste of the wind and the very sound of silence. Those solitary hours, high on Cowpe Moss or Hailstorm Hill, where a babbling stream pulls you back on course on a black night, or in the paling moon you imagine the ghost of a quarryman rising from the black depths of Cheesden reservoir. With eyes glued to the inky waters evil reflections cross your path and you are pulled back to your senses as an unseen ditch claims your balance. One is able to muse with no hindrance. At only sixteen I could cast a mind back to what seemed a lifetime passed. There was talk of another war in Europe now, would my Father have to go again to the saddened fields of Flanders. Perhaps I would go, in two year's time call up age would loom. How much more serious all is becoming. What seemed like yesterday, nothing was important. You didn't consider tomorrow. There was the 'Doctors' man who came round every Friday evening for his five shillings; perhaps he would be out of work if Lord Beveridge's plan went ahead for a National Health Service. Was it only two years ago that we had celebrated the coronation of George the Sixth, and two years prior to that the Jubilee of George the Fifth. Hadn't we all stood in school uniform, waving our little paper Union

Jacks in Whittaker Park and singing a long rehearsed 'Land of Hope and Glory'. Then there were the presentation mugs, and the Yorkshire Penny Bank book with a shilling donated by our Carie Whitehead, the local dignitary. We had school trips to Edinburgh and to North Wales. Now the world was changing. What of the row upon row of uniformed Nazis we see on the Gaumont British news reel. Strutting and shouting 'Sieg Heil' at rallies across Germany. It all appeared ominous. Here was a world about to make a rapid turnabout.

With the rashness of youth however, you think one minute, forget the next. Tomorrow I was to be measured for a suit, the first one that had warranted going along to a tailor's to be measured. My first and previous one had been 'off the peg', but here was the real adult treatment, and the cloth would be 'Air Force Blue', the latest trendy colour. Would they give me a bottle of Brylcreme or a tin of 'Brilliantine' I mused, and then plaster my hair down in the true thirties style.

I had my job on the railway. My career was set, and again I was yearning for the open spaces. Ties with the Rossendale Valley and an affinity to the Rees family had never been severed in any way. By road, track, moor or railway line a close association with all my comrades had been maintained. Now I considered it high time to return to 'wheels' that had been tragically forsaken those few years ago.

So I approached father, now more sympathetic to a son he observed was taking life and its consequences somewhat more rationally, and having recently moved out to Tottington he agreed with my tentative suggestion that it was a more sensible idea to cycle than to walk the three miles to Bury at half past five in the morning, for the start of a six o'clock shift.

Long before there was any chance of a change of heart, I was facing an array of gleaming new bikes stacked against, and inside Frank Aspinall's shop in Kay Gardens. There was little chance of leaving with a Dawes, a Jack Taylor or a Claud Butler. The figure I had saved to was by far insufficient, but there was second hand 'Saxon' with a single gear that caught my eye. It was a prestigious name and that would suit me. By far this was to be the happiest hour I had spent for many a day. I leapt into the saddle and rode pell mell home, and without restraint straight into a disease that would afflict me for many a year to come. .... 'cyclemania'.

CHAPTER 6

SACRED SADDLES

Apart from getting any distance on your feet, or perhaps on horseback, wheels are the prime factor in travel. Buses, trams, trains and even aeroplanes have them. But a cycle is so very different. It has wheels that cost very little to turn, and provides a most economical form of transport. In addition to that, it gives exercise and pleasure of untold wealth. Even today, I find irritability if there isn't a bike somewhere about the house to grab and nip off to the local, or round the villages for a little exercise. Reverting to those pre war years however, we recall no vision of 'jetting' off to far away islands in the sun, or motoring across the continent to countries whose majority of roads were still dirt ones. Indeed, the word 'jetting' had not entered the dictionary. And the thought of motoring within even Britain itself, entered only the mind of the exclusive rich.
Of the bicycle I can but quote Bernard Newman, whose travel books, amongst others, were in heavy demand at the point in time. He says "by bicycle of course. It is easily the most satisfying way of touring. Tramping is good, but limits the country you can cover. A car is hopeless, for you are in a class apart from the ordinary folk in countries where you travel. And buses and trains will not stop and wait on request. You can be off your bicycle in ten seconds should anything of interest chance to come your way. You are in intimate contact with the countryside and its people _ you are accepted more readily as one of themselves. You can stay in village inns, where interesting conversation is available far more readily than in grand hotels. You can keep up a steady fifty or sixty miles a day without effort.'' He later embodies my own sentiments and practises by stating ''The perfect way for one who would learn. With a companion one talks too much and neglects to observe.''
Enshrining these concepts as I polished away madly on my new possession a little voice was whispering. What of those visions of yesteryear; cycle camping in the nearby Pennines or Bowland Forest, riding the lanes of pastoral Cheshire or the limestone uplands of the Yorkshire Dales. With this silent prize on two wheels all had come tantalisingly close.
And now with the prospect of becoming a reality at any time, an added interest came along, and would add zest to any form of travel. That was

the camera. Photography was a passion with my father and he had instilled his enthusiasm for both the taking of pictures and the processing into an ardent observer. The hobby became irresistibly captivating and he offered no objection when I put down a three shilling deposit on a 'Coronet' folding camera and signed to pay the balance of twelve shillings over a period of twelve long weeks. It was my first taste of the dreaded 'never, never'! His dictum on the whole aspects of hire purchase and its potential evils did make me think seriously. At least a curb to smoking was accomplished, and I took to rolling my own cigarettes and even trying a pipe. The shillings added quickly and the results were swift.

In a short time a sectional shed appeared, proudly skirting the edge of our cinder back lane. Inside I built my very first bench and a row of storage cupboards, put up slings to raise the bike. Soon there was cash to buy a three speed, tools for repairs and now the traditional white cycling jacket, and a second hand 'Caradice' saddle bag from my cousin Bert who had been 'called up'. It seemed a war with Germany was fast approaching.

Soon the day I yearned would dawn. But all was not yet ready. To put a second hand bike in a fit state for a long day, or a weekend run was a first priority and lacking a full complement of professional tools it was not the easiest of tasks. A bent crank had been the source of annoyance for the past week and something must be done or likely I would walk with a permanent twist of the ankle.

But the removal of a cycle crank, before ever the splined variations saw the light of day, was just about the most diabolical thing to cross the path of a budding cycle mechanic. The procedure was to upend the bike, place one foot on the handlebars and the other on the upturned saddle. Thus one started work. First the cotter pin is removed deftly with a hammer, hopefully not wrecking the thread because you can't afford a new one, then it's two hands to the pedal to circle the crank in any direction and gradually ease it off the end of the bottom bracket spindle. Quite an easy operation you would say, and it is, providing the two components have been turned and milled to respective perfection. But there are many different manufacturers, and their so called 'standard' fittings DO differ. Certainly the one I was sweating over did, it was no way responsive as I yanked; up, down...up. down...up, down. Bit by bit it evidently was reaching the end but with five minutes gone and no apparent movement I passed into a dreamy stupor. That was when it happened. I could well have been subconsciously bending over to view the operation as they parted company and the crank, swinging freely on the end of the pedal I still held took an accurate line for a point just about one inch above the right eye. The ground came up to meet me in record time and some three minutes later, I was brought back to consciousness by the aid of smelling salts, to raise an eye and see the bulging outline of a lump the size of a duck egg.

This saga of head bashing has haunted me throughout life. It started when I first flew over the handlebars rounding a freshly gritted bend close of Alder Grange School only days after taking possession of my first steed. As seems to be my destiny, the head was first to make contact with the road, and I woke up on that occasion, as I have on many others, with blood trickling to my eyes and the cup of inevitable tea held to the lips. Another kind soul would have dragged me into her house, as they always did.

The bumps were accepted, invariably for some reason they spelled out a run of good luck. And anyway, war had now broken out and I was a little under seventeen; in just over twelve months, I could expect call-up and a lot more bumps and scrapes then. That was if the optimists were proved wrong. The ones that calculated it would all be over in a few weeks.

A 'keep fit' phase had gripped my attentions of late for some reason. It could have been the hackneyed advertisement by Charles Atlas; the one with the 'tough guy' kicking sand into the weedy looking chap's face on the beach. But rather I think it was the inspiration I took from Ted Cox, a signalman I worked under in South Junction Box.

Jogging, or 'scout pace' as it was then known, took my fancy. On the lane from Tottington to Walshaw, my skinny legs would often be seen, that's if there was anyone around, at five in the morning, pounding the pavement prior to cycling to Bury for the six a.m. shift. Admittedly, that pastime was soon forgotten. I found it in no way therapeutic, particularly on a wet or frosty morning, and took a course of exercises, found in an old book by the great wrestler Hackensmidt. These consisted mainly of movements to aid respiration and over the years, I maintained a constant daily fifteen minutes programme. In time to come they would pay me handsomely, particularly in the field of cycle racing.

True to premonition the disease struck. The bike was ever at my side and the next few months found me much a loner. If not at work or browsing among other signal boxes, then I was away to the road. First it was twenty miles, then fifty and finally the hundred in the day. It is at that mileage you first feel you have made it, and class yourself as a seasoned rider. Seldom ever did I use the free pass provided to travel to work by train. Stuffy, smoky carriages were not for me; only the freedom and fitness that came with those beloved two wheels.

Inescapable now, as I knew only too well, would be the magnetic pull of Rossendale, and the pals I'd left behind. Yes, I had walked the road and moor from Bury, even taken the train at times, but here was the situation that they lived almost next door; a mere half hour astride the trusty bike.

Fred had a new 'Sun Vitesse' and Dougy a 'Carlton' and until the war split a world of friends, we were close to an inseparable trio. From the limits of Lancashire and Yorkshire, to the boundaries of Cheshire and Westmorland, the hills and dales would shadow every turn of the pedal. Maps in consequence became a relevant fascination and in time a series from John O'Groats to Lands End came into my possession. I was to use every one. Bartholomew's half inch was the most useful to the cyclist, and before very long these maps would only be obtained at a premium. Signposts across the country were to disappear in 1940 as the threat of invasion heightened and it was jolly hard luck to the traveller who was unable to read a map. Overnight the cloth backed variety disappeared from the bookshops and as far as we were concerned Woolworths were to do a roaring trade selling us calico at sixpence a yard which was then pasted on to the back of any paper backed sheet we could lay hands on. Quite recently, during a hike across the Rooley Moors, Fred and I had scoured the abandoned Moor Cock Inn and amongst debris and a nest of wild cats had unearthed a treasure trove of one inch Ordnance Survey maps. These proved a boon in such time of scarcity and even today, they are still used for reference; roads and footpaths among the high Pennines change little as the years progress.

Armed with such a find our trio had little difficulty in planning a multitude of expeditions, and the likes of Skipton, Settle and Ingleton were our immediate aim. In that direction we would encounter less of the infernal cobblestones that plagued the industrial north.

Though there now arose a frustrating canine problem that we had unwittingly presented ourselves. It was 'Snip'. When the ecstatical moment arrived, and all was set to leap out from Waterfoot to the white walled slopes of Ingleborough and Penyghent, Snip thought he should do likewise. Whenever our group had met in Ivy Street, (that was because Dougy was always the last to get up) Snip had known there was the smell of heather and moors beyond. He had only to catch sight of a rucksack and hell was let loose. Chairs were knocked flying, rugs scattered and chaos reigned. But this was different, saddlebags were not rucksacks, and cycling shoes were not fell boots. Unfortunately, he would have to learn, but it was to be a hard task. We shut him in the back yard, behind a six foot gate and an equally high wall. Nevertheless, at Accrington, seven miles ahead he was bounding alongside. However he knew we had taken that direction, we shall never know: then with typical teenage unconcern we stepped up the speed down Whalley brow a further six miles on, and 'dropped' him. He was back in the house when we returned at night, and this became the practice for well over a year. That he became to know his way home from Rochdale, Bury, Whalley, Burnley and a periphery of towns ten miles from Rossendale was a miracle; a quality I fail to comprehend.

In effect, Snip never was denied his yearning for the open spaces. Interspersed with cycle runs to far away pastures, the boots and rucksacks and our local uplands were deserted never for long. Despite wartime austerities, ration books and the like, overtime and night working, Home Guard and fire watching duties it appeared to have little effect on morale, or the will to get out and enjoy yourself if you could. Even the air raids became a habit. So cycling and an occasional camp at the old haunts was still feasible. On the weekend of May 17th, 1941, camped once again in the unobtrusive hollows of Fern Creek, there was to be flurry of excitement.

At Warth prisoner of war camp to the south of Bury, five hard core Nazi officers had escaped; ingeniously by crawling through a sewer pipe and crossing the Irwell river. But their tracks led the army patrol searchers to the moors, the very ones we were now camped on. All this was an unknown factor to we innocents, so when a frightening challenge was thrown, and we looked up to find a battery of rifles and the nose of a Bren gun poking at us from the top of its tripod, there was consternation all round. Bill Suffell dropped a mug of boiling hot tea into the fire just to shake our nerves a little more. The curses came in a strong Lancashire brogue and the tension eased somewhat. At that point, the boys in khaki lowered their guns and gave us the gist of what had transpired, and we were then given the consequences of spending another night in the open. Although this we did, and learned later the five had been rounded up..... not a few miles from where we camped.

Increasingly it did become frustrating. To be holed up in some moorland hollow alongside a slow flowing peat stream, and suddenly encounter the Home Guard bearing down in delight from a hilltop confidently they had unearthed a patrol of Nazi paratroopers.

With the consequence cycling became more the order of the day. But now and again there are silly rides. Like the one that Fred and I set out on one fine summer's day into the lanes and byways that lace the surrounds of Pendle Hill. It was as we approached Ogden Clough that the challenge loomed. Why not somehow get our bikes on the summit and prove to the world it can be done. And so they were humped, pushed, pulled and at times even ridden on a never to be forgotten scramble to the cairn that marks the summit. All this in order to brag to our mates back home that we had actually done it; and could now produce a photograph to mark the deed. A further gravity defying plunge was made down the northern flank, sometimes riding, sometimes unintentionally sliding and we finished scraping the grit from out of our legs in the charming village of Downham.

Those sorties were by the way, thankfully. And all this hauling of bikes laden with pannier bags and a grossly overloaded saddlebag was becoming irksome. Recently there had been a spate of cycle camping which didn't seem to be turning out anywhere as charming as the contributor to the 'Scout' had forecast. After heaving a mountainous pyramid of weekend necessities attached to a cycle frame up the five mile climb from Gisburn, and again over the wilds of Haslingden Grane I was left wondering. And why the sidelong smirks from passing cyclists who seemed to ride around with nothing more than a cape, a map, and a few sandwiches in a half filled saddlebag. The message we were getting was that they were members of this comparatively new organisation, the Y.H.A., where for the cost of a shilling a night your accommodation was assured. Then for an extra threepence, you had full use of cooking facilities. In good time that would have to be looked into.

For the present however, we had our sights set on a marathon thrust, a spin to Lake Windermere in far off Westmorland. To us at that time, it was elusive; an evocative canvas, seen only on the walls of an L.M.S. railway carriage. There would be little planning. We had a map, but no money; we didn't want weight, so a barn would be a hotel, and we would stuff as many sandwiches as we could in a small saddlebag. Finishing work a two o'clock on a Saturday afternoon, the weekend started well. In Preston, I met up with Dougy and Fred and the jaunt was underway. What I had failed to take into account at that juncture however, was the entire stupidity of what I myself was undertaking. To Windermere and back showed a total of a little under two hundred miles, not unduly excessive for a well trained rider, but as yet, I wasn't in that category, and furthermore for the past five days not a morsel of solid food had passed my lips. Liquid yes; most of it blood. A visit to a dentist suffering from extractamania had witnessed my non too sorry farewell to an entire mouthful of semi decayed teeth. Not that the sight of an eighteen year old face with a gaping wide hole in the middle would worry me, the attractions of the opposite sex had momentarily escaped me. The fact that I had eaten nothing of substance, and the consequential energy rating being just about nil, did produce a few qualms. Nonetheless my buddies were in good form. They carried an ample supply of cheese, peanut butter, and jam sandwiches. Even a tin of baked beans they could bash open with a penknife and eat cold. As for myself, I carried a cape and a repair outfit, the one we shared to save weight, and a brown paper bag with two rounds of bread and margarine. These, I was confident, would be washed down with a mug of cold water.

A fleeting glimpse later from under heavy eyebrows in the vicinity of Lancaster outlined a barn a little off the roadside, so to that we made a thankful dash; at least THEY did; this trembling mass of skin and absent muscle was virtually on the point of collapse. I slept fitfully, but safe in the knowledge that food was in my pocket alongside, and in the morning by hook or by crook, I would force it down..... but the indisious rodent lying alongside and craftily awaiting his opportunity had other ideas, and the molars he sported were sharper than any I would ever again possess. Suffering no inhibitions, or later remorse he took a direct line and tunnelled straight through the gleaming corduroy of my new lumber jacket, through the centre of my cherished 'butties' and out the other side. He even had the audacity to leave behind the framework of the crater he made. That needless to say was flung in anger, in the soft light of dawn. Thank the Lord I had pals to spare a bite.

At six in the morning, we hit the road, and the miles flowed steadily by.

Through Staveley and to the last brow that gives an unforgettable welcome to Lakeland from its summit. From this easily missed vantage point almost the entire length of Windermere can be viewed. To the Langdale Pikes and beyond, westwards towards Coniston and the 'Old Man'. A challenging welcome, that lay only in my subconscious on that day. Sat on a boulder on the lakes edge a little while later, I could have 'eaten a horse'. There was a cheer from my partners, "We're here", and I gave a forlorn smile, and one of them took a photograph. Then we gazed over the lake to banks beyond and I swallowed hard, I'm not sure whether it was awe or hunger. Then the awful realisation struck; we faced a ninety five mile ride home and at six the following morning, I was due at work.

One of them forced half a muffin in my mouth and helped me into the saddle and we were off again. Then for some mysterious reason as dusk approached on the West Riding border a 'second wind' came about and I was treading the pedals like someone on the edge of an epileptic fit. Doug said it happened just before you died; but the laugh was on him as we passed through Settle. He was 'nobbled' as we slid along the shadows with no lights, and the Bobbies scribblings in the notebook cost him the total of seven shillings and sixpence.

The night and the miles rolled relentlessly on and in given time the heights of Deerplay Moor were behind us and we were dropping into Rossendale. In the course of the next three hours I had snatched two hours sleep on the settee at Dougy's house, knocked off the final ten miles, and bleary eyed, rolled into work at six o'clock.

The reader, indeed the prototype of normality would likely say "so that ended your cycling days." On the contrary, it fired even further enthusiasm. The converted, by instinct acquires a thirst for more punishment. As Harry Aspden, a cycling correspondent of high repute penned in a later thesis on the requirements to achieve Olympic greatness, "You must learn to suffer". And that we would in the ensuing years.

With the rolling hills of Westmorland and the craggy heights of Cumberland fresh in my mind, I gazed across from Holcombe to the slopes of Knowle Hill and Scout Moor. They had been my magnet for so long; now they would be forsaken in the quest for lands beyond. Perhaps I would pay my last respects; abandon the new found aspirations and return to the beckoning moorlands. It would be the last camp I was sure; the camp of the pioneer. Not the parody of the present day camper; the camp beds, the gas stoves, the caravans and electric hook-ups and other luxuries of modern times. No, the open fire that makes to search for wood and dry bracken; the hard ground that calls for grass packing under a ground sheet; a place to fry your bacon in the open and curl your fingers in an ice cold east wind, or turn your back to a south westerly gale. To darn your own socks and fend for yourself. A thrill of the backwoodsman when you have staked your claim; pitched your tent and dug the first sod that will mark your fire, and when you leave to spread the ashes, replace the turf and leave nothing behind, but a genuine thank-you.

These thoughts, firmly entrenched set me on course for an old favourite haunt, 'Windy Creek'. Here one could feel an infinity, become and integral part of a world the townsman knows not, and then leave, feeling you had made your peace, with a life you would never know again.

I was glad I was alone. The cyclist who rides alone, the backpacker who walks alone, and the camper who sleeps alone, is never lonely. Far from the noise and bustle of modern life, his friend is contemplation and meditation. My companions were a notebook and a camera. If a fellow human came along he was welcome, if not it mattered little. On the bank of the stream, drifting smoke from a slow burning fire brushing the turf, I could ponder the morrow.

Camp fire cooking had been a fascination, it would stand me in good stead, scouting had instilled a love of the outdoors and now the cycle had become a dominant factor. Without a shade of doubt the open road was calling, and from what I had been hearing of late the Y.H.A. held every answer, to the dreams of an inveterate wanderlust.

CHAPTER 7

TOURING SADDLES

Standing piteously exposed to the mirth of a ring of surprised onlookers, must be the destiny of the one who wears an illfitting mouthful of shining new dentures. Many uproariously funny anecdotes will haunt the wearing, or the wearer of these 'gnashers'. Many have befallen myself, and the consternation of dreams of swallowing them, and awakening in fright, or frantic searches for them under the pillow or deep down in the bed in some remote hostelry can prove infuriating. But the occasion causing maximum of hilarious laughter, to all with the exception of myself, followed a 'belly landing' dive into the swimming baths at Haslingden. The said missiles, only that very day acquired, shot unceremoniously across the offended waters, to sink slowly and clearly, whilst tinkling along the bright tiles and coming to rest at a depth of six feet. And that is a fathom I never cross unless on a bridge or in a boat. Hence Bill Suffle, ever a dry witted individual awaited the glance of his audience, then took a measured and professional dive from the appropriate board and plunged gracefully to the bottom. Three seconds later he surfaced, and with half of Rossendale's swimming community eager for excitement, he threw his arms high, waved the set freely and bawled "got 'em, Ron!" It was not the first time swimming pool panics had assailed. In earlier days, there had been the visit to Bacup Baths with the cubs. Even our cub mistress had commented favourably on the design of my new costume. At the time, boys were not allowed the freedom of trunks, a full costume it had to be, and this one mother had knitted with calculated care, and the wool used reputedly the best. Certainly it was daring, had I been a female; the neckline almost dipped to my nipples. That fact, and the dizzy coloured bands knitted into the design were asking for ribald remarks from a set of noisy chums. Perhaps that's what made me take a hurried dip. Holding thumb and forefinger over my nose, I jumped; and that was into the shallow three feet end, of course. Never would I get a sinking feeling at that depth I knew; but the trouble was the costume DID. Touching the bottom my body steadied, though not the costume; that errant coverage continued to descend in total disregard of conventional decency until the straps on my shoulders narrowed to nothing, and the crotch stretched to my ankles. Now the challenge was to climb out of the water holding a gallon of water trapped within, and at the same time avoid 'little Willie' making his debut in front of a startled young cub mistress. I yanked up the floppy outfit and ran for it to the nearest cubicle. One more quarter of an hour's entertainment for a vociferous bunch of onlookers.

I needn't have worried over the outcome of the affair or the destiny of an elongated heap of wet wool. It turned out to be a source of good value for money; it fitted father to perfection!

The evening's entertainment at Haslingden Baths however, and the subsequent 'feast' in a nearby 'chippie' turned out to be somewhat a farewell party. Within weeks Bill Suffle would be conscripted into the Navy and submarine warfare, whilst Dougy took the uniform of the Royal Marines and would see action in the Normandy landings. David found himself in the R.A.F. and was soon on his way to North Africa; Fred and I alone remained. Despite reserved occupations that kept us working long hours, there was time in hand, and that we used to the best advantage.

The Youth Hostel Association, its membership, its aims and its advantages we fell wholeheartedly into. It was to be an affiliation I enjoyed for six happy years. From the very start the facilities and the camaraderie swept away any worry of the indecision we at first displayed. The impact was tremendous. First we set our target on a week's holiday in the Lake District. To return to the fringes of a magnetism we had felt on that recent day along the shore of Windermere. And so we stowed a trusty 'Carradice', and prepared for our first, week long cycle tour.

The amazing result being, that we had less weight and bulk at the end, than when setting out on a mere weekend's outing over the past few months. Apart from a calico sleeping bag, which purpose was to avoid contact with the hostel blankets; some clean underwear, a cape and repair outfit, map and camera, there was little else to carry. The Y.H.A. did the rest. Food would be purchased as we travelled along and a meal made in the evenings. For a charge of threepence, the facilities were there, and the overnight stop cost merely a shilling. So it went somewhat like porridge for breakfast, bread and jam sandwiches for lunch, and baked beans on toast in the evening; for seven days! In those seven days however, we accomplished a tour of the entire Lake District. We saw every well known strip of water, every famous mountain, and breathed the air on the summit of practically all the best known passes. In truth, Cumbria is a pocket of pure magnificence; England's biggest little corner, and totally unchallengable.

As ever there will be both humorous and frustrating moments when journeying. That's what makes a traveller's wanderings so memorable. On this tour we had not cycled far, when the fun started. The glorious lakes of Crumock Water and Buttermere had just receded to the west and we faced the notorious Honister Pass, with its imposing buttress. Now to tackle the tortuous climb; a gradient of one in four at times; we would see how far up the climb our sturdy legs would take us. At least Fred had sturdy legs; mine, could you have scraped the freckles away would have revealed little more than two thin strips of insignificant tissue. However, they were 'coming on'; time would tell. But for now it was arms lowered, on to the 'drops' and we crouched for the challenge. It would prove a forlorn attempt. At that point it was noticeable that Fred, somewhat shorter in stature than I, was fast rising above my level. He stared aghast, my bike's original wheel base of forty two inches, was fast increasing to an enormous fifty two, and the road surface rising quickly to meet my pedals. There was no need for brakes to stop quickly, gravity did that for us, and I was saved pitching down into an adjacent stream by collapsing full tilt onto my buddy.

At first sight, after extricating ourselves from the shambles, the situation appeared hopeless. It transpired my frame had come apart. Something I've never known happen to anyone since. Resulting from an argument I had with a wall some time previously no doubt. There had been a kink left in the down tube after the forks had been knocked back. Now this had split, leaving a two inch gap in that tube, and a top tube that threatened to bend in half at any time. A splint was attempted but was futile and left us nothing other than to reach the nearest town which was Keswick, and have the thing welded.

I thanked my lucky stars it hadn't happened on the descent from the summit. That was where the huge sign stating "pedal cyclists strongly advised to walk" was glaringly exhibited; I had little chance to do anything other.

Keswick we found was a wonderful town and after browsing round map shops and climbing establishments we returned to the blacksmith's, a little apprehensively, because I had very little money to spare. During our two hour wait however, we had come into conversation with a gentle-man, evidently of some means. He had taken an interest in our travels and invited us to a meal in his hotel. Perhaps he was psychic, for it would be the last occasion I would eat well for several days. The blacksmith relieved me of half a crown, and the net result was that I had money only to pay for the next one night's accommodation.

So from Patterdale Youth Hostel it was, I took the long road home on the final day. Oats there had been enough of just to eke out a last plate of porridge, and with two pence only lodged securely at the bottom of my pocket, I faced Kirkstone Pass and one hundred, long miles south. Only when propping up my bike against a confectioner's window in Lancaster did that awful sensations of a 'hunger knock' drive the last vestige of will from my legs. The magnetic bouquet of freshly baked bread and cakes set up a trembling that had me near to dropping the two pennies. I staggered through the door, and drooled over the two penny dry muffins. They would save me I knew, and they were stuffed into my saddlebag with an effort of will power unknown at that time. The very thought of sitting by the roadside succulently nibbling at those two bastions of British baking was enough to drive the pedals round for another ten flat miles. Then at Garstang I succumbed. With an enamel mug of cold water cadged from a house across the road, I ate a meal fit for a lord. Never in my life has bread and water provided such gastronomic delights. It was a banquet! Enough to see me home by midnight, a welcome bed and visions of counties far and wide looming clear in a proliferary of dreams.

Yes, there were youth hostels twix Lands End and John O'Groats, the majority within riding distance of each other. The field was wide open. There was a membership card with spaces to stamp the evocative names of a multitude of far flung places.

I viewed my bike a couple of days after returning from this first tour of the 'Lakes', as we are prone to address Cumbria. It sported a rough clump of weld the shape of an ill battered golf ball; and this, in such a glaringly obvious location did little to enhance the prestigious name of 'Saxon'. Neither did it instil a height of confidence in its rider. Although it had faithfully carried me from Cumbria to South Lancashire, its luck could run out again.

That is where my brother Cyril came onto the scene. Approaching school leaving age, he himself was taking a keen interest in the antics of his cycle crazy elder kinsman, and now he saw a rapid method of augmenting the pennies he was saving to one day buy a bike himself. It appeared that on a rubbish dump he had recently been scavenging along with his young pals, he had come by a discarded bike that although in a state of total unridability, had displayed a likely useable frame. And he was correct. He stripped the unwanted accessories and thrust the frame in front of me at a most opportune moment; I think that was pay day. I was delighted, it was admirable, and how much did he want for it? One and sixpence he suggested; so we haggled a while and settled for an even sum of one shilling, five pence in today's calculations!

It came to be the best shillingsworth I've ever purchased in my life. By the time I'd scraped it, painted it, and varnished it; then added artistically the letters A.S.P.; denoting all spare parts, it was beginning to look almost professional. The wheels were transferred, along with all other necessities, and oil and grease added here and there to produce what appeared virtually a new machine. Over a period of the next six years, that converted piece of scrap metal would carry me a total of over 85,000 miles. Much more than the average motorist travels today. From the highlands of Scotland to the coves of Cornwall that trusty steed steered me, and if ever an old piece of junk deserved a medal, then that was the one.

Significantly money, or the doubtless lack of it, contributes a large deal in the pursuit of pleasure in these modern times. Not so in the times of 'make do and mend', and self created entertainment. For as little cost as the rubber I wore off my tyres, I could well spend a superb day in the country. Setting out alone to cover a distance of 150 miles perhaps, I would have stuffed a sixpenny piece in my pocket. It was merely a token. In all probability, it would still be there on return. According to my log of the period, a one day's jaunt may start from home with an ample supply of sandwiches and an aluminium flask of cold tea clipped to the frame. There would be little else to carry but map, tools and camera and the day could well take in Whalley, Settle, Ingleton, Hawes, Kettlewell and Malham, with a tramp to the summit of Pen-y-Ghent thrown in. A homeward thrust and a glowing exhilaration that tones the mind, then a sun tanned skin to challenge the housebound. All that, and not having parted with a penny along the road.

About this time the hostel, Jerusalem Farm, was becoming a firm favourite. In particular, because the warden, a Mr. Gummershall was extremely co-operative when it came to bending the rules. These state that members should have booked in, and finished their evening meals and the like much before ten o'clock in the evening; but on every other Saturday evening, that was precisely the time I was finishing work, some thirty five miles distant. Mr. Gummershall was sympathetic and conse- quently the opportunity was not missed. It saw me often changing railway uniform for shorts and sweater in South Signal Box at Bury and charging off at full pelt in the dark to Jerusalem Farm, where the creepy appellative 'Midnight Rider' was subsequently bestowed. At least it held a distinguishing ring that I preferred to the tags such as 'the one with the skinny legs and red hair' or 'the bloke with the mouth organ'. It became symbolic, that with this title I could often have been seen shinning up a drainpipe at two in the morning to request a clandestine entry through some dormitory window, or be pounding the byways of North York- shire long after the hour of an accepted bedtime.

Many of these escapades were purely a result of attempting the virtually impossible. Far too many miles were eaten up in an attempt to widen our horizons; to taste the delights of Derbyshire, Staffordshire, and Shrop- shire were our weekend targets, and next the border counties of Flintshire and Denbighshire in Wales, would come. Given a map to scour, and a hostel available, we were to take up the challenge, and all were within range. natural progression you would say; and this is where Derwent Hall, and one of the coldest December weekends I can recall enter the scene.

Derwent Hall, lying deep in the folds of the Peak District and not far from the bluffs of Kinder Scout was high on our agenda of 'musts'.

It was the ultimate goal of both Fred and myself.

The urgency being that before very long, the imposing edifice was to languish under the deep waters of a further reservoir in the chain required for the use of Nottingham City.

As ever we insisted on wearing shorts. It was not only that it was fashionable, it was sheer bravado, and superseded all rational thought. In sub zero temperatures like these, why ever we didn't consider what would be the results of that ruthless east wind blowing up, and directly through, what little protection we had, I fail to understand. To find anything at all, in the way of a male attachment when the call of nature arose, was a task of concentrated agony. We swore they had dropped off.

On the summit of Snake Pass, one of the earliest of the Pennine passes to block in heavy snow at any time, we all but perished; it was too cold to even ride down the other side. We just walked, and shivered, and when the lights of Derwent Hall eventually showed through the hoarforest it was sheer ecstasy. Through the portals of this baronial mansion, and over the threshold, instinct raised our feet; we weren't sure they were still attached to our frozen limbs. And the glow of a massive log fire, enclosed in a surround of enormous proportion drew us like a magnet. Then, as we stood alternately shivering and convulsing the warden strode across. He would have been better placed in a Nazi concentration camp. He was adamant; no, the hostel was booked up; every bed was taken, and no, we couldn't sleep on the floor, that was unheard of in his domain of rigid authority; and he goosestepped back to his office. We, trembling, stepped outside again.

On the way out a sympathetic inmate had whispered we may 'get in' at the pub down the road, but we carried insufficient money for that form of luxury. Nevertheless, we could have a look in and warm our bones whilst we thought up some scheme or other; certainly the vision of burrowing into a heap of hay in some remote barn brought no form of solace on a night like this. So into the little pub at Ashopton, now itself beneath the Pennine waters, we crept. I say crept because in effect, we were attempting an inconspicuous guise. With barely enough money to spare for a 'gill', the intention was to eke it out as long as possible while toasting our feet and knees, and at the same time seeking inspiration.

We were in luck. About half way through the Sheffield ale, and able to co-ordinate mind and body, an American pushed through the crowd to come and sit alongside us; he was curious, we didn't look at all the average 'Brit' sitting there on a freezing cold night in shorts and ankle socks. So we eased our chairs back all of two inches from the fire and got into conversation. First our tale of woe was unfolded and he raised a sympathetic eyebrow. It appeared he was an engineer working on the dam project, and the viaduct that was straddling the valley, directly behind the pub. His wife was in charge of the workmen's accommodation which consisted of a series of wooden chalets built alongside, and over that particular weekend, most men were away. Would we care to be his guests and stay overnight? Perhaps enjoy a late meal, and in the morning there would be English breakfast; eggs, bacon and sausages. We certainly wouldn't be cold he pronounced, there were ample wool blankets and a wide choice of eiderdowns! How could we refuse. It would have been both impolite and, under the circumstances, extremely imprudent. From then on the weekend turned out to be a resounding success.

In time a dozen or more of these Derbyshire Y.H.A. strongholds would claim a rendez-vous, either by cycle, or on foot.

Pounding the pedals in hitherto unexplored counties had become all but an obsession, though to the likes of two lads born twix high hill and moorland it would take more than the pull of the glistening highroad or the thrill of a swoop down a mountain pass to have us forsake our boots and rucksacks.

As ever accompanied by Fred, we alternated our weekends with an occasional tramp deep into the grasslands of Bronte fame, and it was during one of these weekend hikes and whilst staying at Jerusalem Farm that we first came into contact with a merry crowd from Bolton. It was a meeting of significance, for several of them became lifelong friends. The likes of Ron Booth, Sally and Margorie, Bill Smethurst and several others. Initially it was a comparative short association, due to the war, but teaming up with this group brought us a host of happy times. Whether walking or cycling the easy rapport made light the many tribulations of wartime travel. It could be a choking smokescreen across Accrington, the 'black out' on a particularly foggy night and the aggravations of trying to pick out the outlines of a jay walker with a half screened headlamp; or the absence of a signpost and the silent curses when you find four miles along the road that it is the wrong one. There may be searchlights raking the sky over Manchester or its suburbs, and the rumble of guns or the whine of a falling bomb as you near home again, and you wonder will you find your street and your family are gone. They were the expectation in wartime Britain, but at least a strong sense of camaraderie went a long way to easing the frustrations and anxieties, a battered Britain that few will now remember. Long hours and hard work deterred no-one. Given just a couple of hours to spare in an evening there were the dance halls or the pictures. With us, it was inevitably the clubroom of this Bolton group, and if my memory serves me correctly that lay somewhere in the vicinity of Bridge Street.

It came about during one of our meetings that I was overheard making plans for a lone cycle tour in the highlands of Scotland. In a week's time my annual seven days leave was due, although the month was yet only

April. Little expecting any response, that if anyone else was due for holidays so early in the season, they were welcome to accompany me. It came as a surprise then when up shot a lad by the name of Gordon who I had never met before, and said if there was any chance at all he would come. So an amended itinerary went ahead.

Neither of us had ever seen the Highlands. The nearest I had ever been to those far away territories was to Edinburgh on a school rail trip. Now was my chance. Working on the railway gave me the advantage of a yearly free pass and that could be used as far as the L.M.S. railway extended. In this case it was to Oban on the west coast of Scotland, and why not go as far as I could with that asset, and cycle the long journey home. That was settled and Gordon was in full agreement, he was only too glad to have found someone to go off with.

Synonymous with my love of the railways it was galvanising to find ourselves boarding a night express to Perth, and hauled by non other than the ''Duchess of Rutland'', rumbling into Wigan station at the hour of midnight in all its streamlined splendour. Indeed it was a novel way to start a cycle tour, but the ways of a railway devotee are uncommon to those of normal habit.

We had our first glimpse of the Braes and a feel of the land of Rob Roy McGregor from the carriage of a Highland railway train north of Stirling, then at mid-day we arrived at Oban to claim bikes from the guards van, and head north to the evocative grandeur of Glencoe; land of the clan McDonald.

Up to then, I had never seen such majestic country, this was so vast. And to cycle along the banks of sea, loch and coast, and to see snow on the peaks whilst stripped to the waist, was a new and invigorating experience. The Scottish hostels too proved excellent and we were only to regret the short duration of time that gave us but two days in this most fabulous region. There were six days to ride home and time would not wait, so from the grandeur of the Buchaille Etive Mor and the wilds of Rannoch Moor we rode south, to the softer lands of Peebleshire and the border. By Loch |Lomond and the Trossachs, to the glorious city of Edinburgh. Not far from here the grim castle of Blackness on the Firth claimed a one night stay, fascinating to say the least, but ever there was a schedule to keep and wheels must roll southwards. Over the scenes of border frays at Carter Bar and to the wild expanse of Northumberland to Hadrians Wall and Hexham. Through the delightful city of Durham and the charm of Barnard Castle, and so on to our final overnight stop at Kettlewell, picturesque and tranquil, resting on the banks of the Wharfe in North Yorkshire.

Pre-arranged the meeting had been, and all worked to plan. Within minutes of arriving here in rolled our nine colleagues and it was a great reunion. As if we had been absent for a year; but such ventures were rare indeed at the time, and by time for 'lights out', all our experiences and anecdotes had been related, and in high spirits they were already planning their own onslaught north of the border for the annual 'wakes' in June.

In all probability it had been this long thrust from the confines of central Britain that gave me the idea of projecting clearly all the roads I had covered by cycle on a huge ten inch to the mile map, I had recently acquired, and pasted on to a large sheet of cardboard. These were clearly defined by the use of black ink and the treasure was hung by a string on the bedroom wall. The upshot was another challenge, almost becoming a further obsession; to mark in as many new routes as was humanly possible, and no stone was left unturned. If there was an alternative road irrespective of a five mile detour, it was taken, and religiously marked in. By the time the monstrosity, which seemed to be perpetually in someone's way, and bounced from one bedroom to another, and from attic to cellar, had crumbled into non existence, there were blackened lines from the North of Scotland to the tip of Cornwall and from the east coast to the west at a staggering variety of points.

It could have been the attraction of 'eating up the miles', the affliction of the time that set my eyes wandering in the direction of a tandem.

For the event I saved hard, and with fourteen pounds bought a second hand machine complete with hub brakes and a 'Trivelox' three speed derailer gear. It was in addition to the 'solo', and took up an enormous amount of room in the shed, but proved a worthwhile investment. There would be cherished adventures as time unfolded.

Cyril, my brother was showing a keen interest now, and would be first to take honour of the back seat. Soon we learned the art of synchronisation that benefits a good team of two, and across the flat highways of Cheshire and south west Lancashire we churned up the miles. In the hills, there was the fearsome thrill of a breakneck swoop, to the valley below, smoke bellowing from a burning hub disc, and the fleeting glimpse of a frightened motorist as you overtake him in his little Austin Seven.

The others watched; and waited. They would all have their turn. After Cyril came Jimmy Revell, Tom Hamer and Ron Booth. With Ron, I don't know whether it was his idea or mine, we set off and rode the two hundred miles to Shrewsbury and back; just to say we'd done it! The trouble was, that as on so many occasions, I dropped them off at their homes, they tucked into a hearty supper and I was left trundling a half manned steed a further ten miles to base. Bill Smethurst bought a tandem himself, Fred Rees would later follow, but there were more still to hop on to the back of my trusty machine, as time went by. In time, there was Dough Taylor, Laura Robinson and every one of the Rees offsprings. Each would face the delights or agonies as the case may be, and the last of that happy household, the Rees's would travel the farthest; because she married me.

CHAPTER 8

TWIN SADDLES

It must have been dedicated love, because the hair raising escapades we went through together both on that tandem, and the solo I built her before the wedding bells jingled were tantamount to divorce before marriage. But the young 'Dot', the one who argued with a lampost in her earlier days and who had also experienced the indignity of falling into the river below Cowpe dye works, and being fished out resembling a psychedelic bundle of waste cloth, was built of stern British tenacity. She was soon to learn the 'hard riders' axiom, ''don't say die until you're dead''.

At this juncture Fred, who had met Nora, sister of Brenda Greenhalgh and close friend of Eva Benson of the Rochdale Y.H.A. group was suddenly faced with his call up papers. Shortly he would be away to join the Navy which left the old stalwarts sadly depleted, and myself glued to a reserved occupation. The railway marshalling yards were now my posting for twelve hours of every day or night. Yet there still came time for limited pleasures.

Almost a natural progression found me teaming up with Dorothea following Fred's twentieth birthday, and a farewell party. The erstwhile 'little' green eyed sister of my best friend was changing rapidly my wanton eyes had discovered. Her shapely legs would turn a nifty pedal at the rear of the tandem I suggested, and so it came about. A happy foursome consisting of Ron Booth, Laura Robinson, myself and Dorothea was seen frequenting a multitude of hostels across the United Kingdom from that point in time.

The first thing Dorothea did on turning her attention to the world of the cyclist, was to snatch avidly at the 'Cairns' frame offered by big brother, and hand it over to me to add the rest; thus another 'A.S.P.' was born. The situation was admirable. You take your choice, tandem or solo, dependent on circumstances that were normally dictated by the terrain. For her initiation into the wonders of cycling however, we had no choice, it had to be the tandem, and away the foursome went to Dacre Banks youth hostel on the fringe of the 'Dales'. As glorious a weekend in spring as anyone would wish.

In Wensleydale the cascading charms of Aisgarth Falls went by, and then the lure of the Town of Hawes. Finally, I must allow her the stark magnetism of of the hamlets of Keld, and Upper Thwaite in Swaledale, so close it would be sacrilege to avoid. The 'Buttertubs' loomed ahead. So named due to the fascinating limestone strata existing alongside this pass between the two dales. But the climb is notorious, and a curse when a tandem needs dragging up the one in four climb. Should I care? No, the gallant Ron would sweat and heave, and display his nonchalance to a hopeful convert; ..... anyway the plunge into the valley of the Swale was to come. It would be our last stop before taking the Howgills, and the plains to the south beyond.

In effect, it nearly WAS our last stop, the high stone wall facing us at the foot of the steep drop loomed menacingly ahead and sheep were scattering wildly as we hurtled headlong down. It seemed to have become a habit with this machine, that a full minute was required to burn out the oil from the brake linings after the levers had been pulled tight to the handlebars, then a wild skid would take over on the back wheel and all but pitch the two riders into the undergrowth. Anyway from the ecstatic cries behind me Dorothea appeared to be enjoying it all. She mistakenly understood I had full control of the monster, and when the brakes did eventually bite and we halted two feet from the threatening masonry, her cheeks were still red; MINE were white; SHE was laughing her head off whilst I smothered an apprehensive grin. I didn't doubt now she was one of us!

Given the weight of a tandem, and its extra wide tyres, the crossing of tramlines and the incessant vibrations of unending cobblestones had the aggravation somewhat minimised. There were some twenty five miles of those monuments to an industrialised irritant between Rossendale and Cheshire town of Hazel Grove. The town I am sure that took its emotive title when they split the road here in two and sent one to the charms of North Staffordshire and the other to the delights of Derbyshire; and covered each one with that celestial surface of velvet, known then as 'tarmacadam'.

In consequence, the attractions of Derbyshire and the Peak District were now to the fore. Though for some unknown reason almost each and every penetration brought its share of trepidation. If a dynamo lighting set was going to throw in the sponge, it would be half way down Winnets Pass, a puncture on the bleak uplands of Axe Edge or a cable snapping and finding us careering down Long Hill and through the first set of traffic lights in Buxton showing red. All three brakes could be glowing hot on the mad descent of Snake Pass into Glossop where every tortuous bend gave its share of palpitations. Impervious to the consequences however, we still craved more, until our quest for thrill was finally dampened on the slopes of Mam Tor, the 'moving mountain'. Now gone forever are the hairaising double bends that plagued the traveller on this geological phenomenon. But this time we didn't have time to look, coming into the first of the hairpins it was quite obvious we would not make it. Neither of the two hub brakes were biting and the one caliper at the back was in effect next to useless, we were still picking up speed. By then, our colleagues some way behind witnessed the pair of us astride the cross bars sliding all four feet until the very soles of our shoes threatened to disintegrate. And before the inevitable happened I shouted 'jump' at about forty miles an hour, and we flung ourselves onto the embankment. In effect, we suffered little more than a few superficial bruises, and there was the minimum of blood letting. Even our trusty steed was little the worse. After hauling it back up from a six inch ditch, extricating the derailer mechanism from the spokes and jumping about on a buckled wheel, the 'faithful' returned us to the land of factory chimneys once more.

Another year had passed by and the annual seven day holiday presented yet another opportunity to thrust far afield. This time I was alone and the time of the year, late spring. Decidedly my purpose now was to strike into the unknown, and at the same time add more to that long elusive black line from Lands End to John O'Groats. With vivid recollections of the charms of the Wye Valley I had read of late, it was to Chepstow at the confluence of the Severn and the Wye that now became my target.

Once more the cherished 'free pass' proved a boon. With that I took the train to South Wales and spent the week exploring the Wye from estuary to source, taking in the delightful town of Ross and Hereford in England, and the picturesque Welsh towns of Builth Wells and Rhayder on the higher reaches of this extremely pleasant river; then known well as the very cleanest in the country.

From where Plynlymmon springs the first waters of the Wye and Severn the roads unfold to hills of green. Through the western fringe of Cymric Britain, Merioneth and Caernarfon. There my wheels took me, and into the bastions of Snowdonia then the lush meadows of Cheshire, and subsequently home. Altogether an admirable exercise, and once more a confirmation, that he who travels alone need never be lonely.

Unfolding the delights of North Wales to the little band of followers appeared to herald a consensus of opinion that our weekend jaunts should strike further afield. Gladys, the elder of the Rees household and an ex Rossendale Wheeler expressed a reborn interest in tagging along, and for a little while the mileage attempted had little respect for the outset time of three o'clock on a Saturday afternoon. To our sorrow, it appeared none of the wardens, in charge of these distant hotels had ever heard of the 'midnight rider'. As instance when we rolled into the village of Gyffylliog, deep in the Clwydian hills of Wales at twelve thirty in the morning. Following a discreet tapping on the door of a slumbering warden we were subjected to a torrent of indecipherable Welsh from within the grey slate walls. My knowledge of the language of the Cymru is extremely limited, but I was left in little doubt that he was NOT calling "diolch yn fawr", the English equivalent of 'thank you very much'!

With Dorothea and on a marathon run to Scarborough on the east coast the return stop was to be at Kirkby Malzeard, a hostel tucked away in a sleepy village on the western side of the plain of York. It had been a foul west wind that we strove against and the church clock had barely peeled the last stroke of midnight as we bumped through the cobblestoned yard. Once more came my expertise in the art of shinning up a drainpipe, crossing a precarious slope of roof tiles, and tapping on the men's dormitory window with the utmost of discretion. The snag this time, was that it was not the dormitory of the visiting traveller, but the bedroom of the warden himself. He was snoring heartily and I did think it peculiar at this time; HIS was the only snore emitting from that one room.

It seemed we had once more discovered the acquaintance of an individual in no way captivated by the antics of an unorthodox band of happy hostellers from the likes of Manchester. He flung up the window, stuck a key into m y hand and pointed cross into the gloom, where the outline of a decrepit building was barely visible; "You'll be in there" was his curt comment. "Get yourself a blanket from the cupboard and I'll see you in the morning". And with that he slammed down the window.

To make matters even worse, I lost my footing on the icy roof, and broke a half dozen tiles plummeting to the ground. All in an effort to make a little LESS noise. We crept into the building across the yard, surveyed the two dormitories after spending five minutes searching for the light switch which didn't exist, because, the place was lit by oil lamp. They were empty. The eerie light of a waxing moon was sufficient anyway, and we climbed a couple of stairs to the mysterious blanket cupboard. All was as silent as the grave, and I turned the handle curiously, something made me do that; then there was pandemonium; a body, that of a very much alive human crashed to the floor, picked itself up and fled through the door wrapped only in a blanket

and very little else. Dorothea, even in flight HAD observed it to be a male.
By the time we had helped ourselves to what covers we needed and gone to
our respective dormitories, I noted the cause of our palpitations was safely
snoring away on a bunk bed, and most evidently the erstwhile sole occupant
of the hostel; his reason for the cosy sojourn in the confines of a blanket
cupboard, I assumed.

In retrospect, I am amazed how smoothly the organisation of these
weekend gathering came about. The four, and sometimes six of us lived
as far as twenty miles apart from each other, and telephone communi-
cation was impossible for none of us possessed one. It was a case of
parting one weekend and after making a quick decision of what hostel
appealed to us, meeting up somewhere along the road the following
week. From Bolton, Bury, Rochdale or Rossendale all would roll up at
some convenient point; invariably Walkden memorial if we were heading
south or Whalley toilets if we were striking to the north. As if by magic
or hypnotic suggestion all would converge within ten minutes of the
suggested time.

Whatever our laurels in the field of organised departures, the curse of an
underestimated headwind and a drastically over ambitious mileage
would ever haunt our merry little band.

It was not always the case of shinning up a drain pipe or trusting to the
sympathies of a co-operative warden. Often we never even reached our
desired hostel in the first place.

In a howling gale on the barren wastes of Tan Hill moor four of us
abandoned the road to Alston and took a night's refuge in an abandoned
car about one in the morning. The hostel we had been aiming for was
Masham, but somewhere on that black night beyond Swaledale all went
wrong, and we cursed Adolf Hitler as the cause of not a single signpost
left on the few roads that straddle the backbone of England.

On the slopes of Dummail Raise a barn again gave shelter to three
exhausted optimists who found the walls of Keswick hostel well beyond
their reach on the hour of midnight. And at first light the wheels rolled again
and a sympathetic warden stamped the cards after a subtle offer of double
'duties'.

Not only were there blunders in the calculations of latent muscle power
for the outward journeys; often the anticipated time of return sorely
misjudged and often well in advance of the late evening; more often than
not it would be in the early hours of the day following. Such a situation

arose on a visit to a staunch favourite, Scar Top hostel in upper Wharfedale. One of these weekends when nothing goes right.

It started at Tottington where I then lived. Having decided that just to add variety to the foursomes little adventures this weekend Laura would take the rear of the tandem whilst Dorothea and Ron would ride 'solo'. And Laura arrived by solo, following her fifteen mile ride from Chorley, to find all ready. She dumped her bike in my shed and we were off in good style; a few rolls until she got the feel of tandem riding, but that I was used to. In Rossendale we met with Dorothea and in Skipton, with Ron. Luck was in, with a roaring south west wind on our backs and we were making record time at Kilnsey Crag, the limestone mass that dominates this sector of the Wharfe. Only then did the chain of events take an untoward course, first with the camera taking a dip in the river, unintentionally, that is.

Always, I am seeking some unlikely position in which to angle an unorthodox shot, and a cluster of boulders way out in the fast flowing river offered a tempting vantage, but the green, moss covered stones that were to pass under my feet had other ideas. The thin leather strap to my camera had long since disintegrated and with the prized possession gripped tight in my hand, the inevitable happened. Down I went into three feet of swirling water and the camera sailed forth in disgust to settle in a deep pool six feet beyond. Although I rescued it in substantially little time the worst was feared. Nevertheless, on later examination both camera and exposed film were in excellent condition, and a tribute to some precision workmanship.

But more was to come. With the precious patrimony strapped tight to the tandem's pannier frame, and dripping the phosphorescent waters of the Wharfe onto the roadside, we approached a grit strewn fork in the road near the village of Kettlewell. That was when we learned the overall advantage of re-checking all nuts and bolts a second time after carrying out some adjustment or other. Apparently, this fact had escaped attention. As is understandable the disadvantage of partnering a variety of willing souls on your dual and bisexual steed, is that you will have a multiplication of leg lengths to cater for, and the consequential highering and lowering of the seat pillar to adjust. When you have done this the important thing to do is tighten the threaded nut, and tighten it well. This is what had not been done, and Laura, a little taller than the last lucky person, and a girl with an eyecatching leg and a sturdy frame, was a picture of tranquillity as we approached the corner, a girl with a smile to enchant the most dreary; that was immediately before we hit the pothole. When we did the consequence was uproariously funny; had you have been the spectator..... Down went the saddle with a thud, her feet both shot from the pedals and at the same time both hands from the handlebars. In no way could I control the careering machine, we came into the corner and onto the evil grit, leaning at a hopeless angle and in seconds the machine was scythed recklessly from under us. When they picked us up it was a miracle they found no broken bones.

Bloodstained and impregnated with road grit we turned into the hostel yard. The girls went ahead, they knew their way. Ron and I unstrapped the bags and followed a while later. WE knew the way too; we'd been so often. There was no need to read signs and notices and we struggled the bags upwards and into the men's dormitory..... We opened the door and walked in. But it wasn't the men's dormitory; it was the females'. We were well inside when we dropped the luggage and lifted our eyes. It was spellbinding. We were transfixed to the spot. They told us afterwards it was intentional, but it wasn't; it was pure shock. This had always been the men's dormitory. Now there were girls cavorting around in scanty underwear, and some without. No doubt they were running for what little cover there was, and the vision is still etched clearly in my mind. It is to be remembered all this was long before the age of liberation and freedom from inhibitions that came with the swinging sixties.

How were we to have known the dormitories had been changed over the week previously? That particular tableau was the only joy I cherished in a prolonged night of ache and pain until morning arrived, and we were back astride the bikes.

It seemed though we had not suffered enough. We struck further north to the wilds of upper Teasdale and the impressive fall of Cauldron Snout, then about turned to face that cruel sou'wester that was never to let up on the hard grind south. Mile after mile it was sheer purgatory, that until I faced the tandem down the last drop before home. It was two in the morning and Laura breathing in stentorian tones behind me was evidently a shade only from death's door. I flattened out for the descent and commenced to freewheel, taking every advantage; Stubbins Brow I knew every inch of and was ready for the bend at the foot, just opposite my Uncle Edwin's. But an uncanny rocking had set up and only in the nick of time the realisation struck me; Laura was asleep. A quick flip of the pedals brought her round in time, and how we avoided a nocturnal trip into Turnbull's mill yard on that black night I shall never cease to comprehend.

Twenty minutes later we were home; or at least I was. I took Laura's bike from the shed, helped her onto it, and she wobbled away into the night. I felt I would never see her again, and the premonition proved rightly so. It was the closing of an album of misfortunes.

In the same vein, I think of other stalwarts who have jumped astride the saddle 'at the back'. Gladys comes to mind. Again the day was one notorious in its ever discourteous method of reminding one the direction of our island's prevailing winds. In other words, it was a stinking rotten sou'wester once again. Two enjoyable days in the dales, from Ingleton to Keld, and from Richmond to Ripon were behind us when we took the brunt. On the flat expanse of the Vale of York we were into the teeth of it and from the seat of her solo, Gladys, crouched low in the saddle looked ahead at her sister, at all appearances having an easy time of it at the rear of the tandem.

In truth that is not the case. Much practice is needed to attain unison and harmony in the art of tandem riding. And with certainty one will soon be aware if the other is not pulling his or her weight.

Gladys nonetheless possessed wonderful powers of persuasion. At the next tea and toilet stop she had worked her spell. Dorothea was to have the honour of a ride on the now vintage 'Parlight', and Gladys would achieve her long cherished ambition; to sit blissfully at ease, nonchalantly gazing at the passing countryside from the secure confines of a tandem rear seat.

We took off into the wind again; tandem first and the rest echeloned to take maximum shelter. It was hardly a time for practice though, and there were a few rolls as I endeavoured to counteract the tugs on the handlebars behind. A new rider has to learn NOT to attempt to steer from the back, and with a wind like that blowing my calls went unheeded. Then came the first traffic island. We came in at a reasonable speed and I set the lean as the bollards neared, but the trouble was that the 'solo' rider on the back, inexperienced did likewise, and in the split second two right pedals struck the kerb side and the back wheel reared like a broncho. How we kept the machine upright is a mystery. Those following up to now, eager to take every advantage of shelter from a faster machine, found it now prudent to battle into the wind alone, and give us a wide berth, they left us to gaze ruefully at a couple of bent cranks, and decide the art of tandem practice should be left until a more appropriate time.

At our next stop, unscheduled, but on Blubberhouses Pass, the wind did it for us, the two sisters happily reverted to their respective saddles and the experiment was finally over.

What this last battle with the elements, and the nature of the terrain had taught me, finally convinced us that tandems were not made for the Yorkshire Dales, or the likes of any heavy country for that matter. They were a machine for the highways of the plains, and with Scotland now in mind again, it would be a case of back to the 'solos' once more.

CHAPTER 9

GETTING SADDLED

The last of our very close friends, Ron Booth was the latest to depart. The R.A.F. and some airfield in distant Penang in Malaysia were awaiting him. For us the wedding bells were looming closer and we were now alone. Annual leave came round once again, this time in July and I would show Dorothea as much of Scotland as was possible in those seven short days.

As in each of the past few years, bikes were stowed in a railway guards van. This time it was an express to Glasgow.

It is a stone's throw only to Loch Long, to the Gareloch and to the braes and banks of bonny Loch Lomond, then to the glens of the western Grampians. If ever a country would cast a spell on me, then it was this land of eternal mountain, of lake, and the purple of the heather. Perhaps it was the ribbon my father handed down to me. A mysterious piece of tartan to be attached to the christening robe of each succeeding first born male. A hint maybe of the dark deeds of the Duke of Cumberland, and the banning of the name McGreggor. And the return of the scattered remnants of a fallen Scottish army that cast its stragglers in the folds of the hills of northern England, to change their names, or face the lance.

The bewitchment interfused; my fiance had the blood of the Cambro-Britain and succumbed. From Ben Cruachen of the Campbells, along Loch Awe to the misty outlines of Jura, and from Oban to Ballahulish she found enchantment. Alas, at Glencoe there was incantation..... and she would put foot on the ground where the Clan McDonald were callously massacred.

Glencoe youth hostel stood proud. I remembered it well from my last stay. The Scandinavian structure was of modern design and its facilities were faultless, but the immaculate edifice was hostile, and its warden a severe spectacle that was foreign. No favours for sure would pass the hand of this formidable character.

Hopefully none would be needed. When a fellow hosteller suggested a visit to the scene of the massacre of his ancestors, we saw no need to request any late pass, should there even have been one; there were two long hours to spare.

But time is of no essence in the brooding dusk that evokes spirits of marauding Hanovarian 'red coats' and treachery of the 'Red Fox'. Wild cats call from the bastions of rock that tumble from the high crags of the 'Three Sisters', and these in turn echo a haunting resonance as their waters plunge into the glen below. Glencoe and the field of the massacre are no place for the faint hearted in the black of night.

And night it was now, as we returned; we stumbled over rocks and waded a stream. None of us had a watch and we sensed the worst as a black and silent hostel loomed through the trees. It was close to midnight. "I'm going through here" said 'Jock' and disappeared through the men's dormitory window which he had doubtless earmarked before the excursion went under way; that was on ground level, but it happened the women's dormitory that Dorothea wanted, was high on the second floor, and all that offered assistance was a pigeon ladder, flush against the wall. In all probability, a fire escape. This held no attraction to her whatsoever, but after a whispered encouragement from 'Jock' leaning through the window, and myself with a shoulder to her posterior, she made all of six steps upwards; Then plummeted back down in sheer panic. There wasn't even a moon to cast a glimmer of light on that vertical death trap, and the webs that criss crossed lay unseen and unbroken; until the hair of our human predator snapped them.

The terrified spider ran down her back and was gone, and I was left brushing a tangle of its mesh from her hair. And that little experiment was over ;"Bring her through the window here" suggested 'Jock'. "The lads are all asleep..... we'll sneak her out and through the common room to the stairs." She had little option; with a shove from behind, and a yank from inside, she was through, and straight onto the top of a snoring Glaswegian. HIS muffled complaints were soon snuffed with a pillow, and we crept across to the door for a cautious peep into the common room, but out luck was out. Directly across, and sat serenely behind his office desk was our protagonist, the dreaded warden.

So we waited, and we waited. Would he ever go to bed? Dorothea trembled, not with cold but with fear. What if she were found; a completely innocent girl taking clandestine refuge in a bedroom full of Highlanders whose reputation to a Sassenach from the lowlands of England was deemed other than honourable to a stray maiden.

Then within half an hour the tension eased. Visions of a commandeered membership card and the repercussions associated dissipated. The warden's light was snuffed; he arose and crossed to his private rooms. All was quiet. We allowed five minutes and then she was gone; I prayed she wouldn't crash into some unseen table or a chair. But all went well; the minute squeak of a closing door, and then ethereal silence. All was well.

From Rannock Moor and the shores of Tummel, the magic of the Trossachs pulled us eastwards, then the braes alongside Loch Katrine and Achray; Scotland's finest scenery, and close to the grave of the redoubtable Rob Roy, a new romance was sealed. No longer were we cycling companions alone, a lifelong bond was forged.

In October of the same year, we joined hands in the Church of Saint Annes, alongside the school that had given me such pleasure as a child, the cub room that gave birth to my yearning for travel, and tragically the grave yard, that would make claim the frail body of our first born.

Entrenched in these early days of wedlock it was only to be expected that outdoor activities would take a back seat, if only for a restricted time. My work called for a return to the Rossendale Valley and a home was found thereabouts following a short time in lodgings. In modern times you would hardly class it a house; merely a home with four walls. It stood on the hillside, a cluster of sixteen 'back to back' properties named 'Primitive Terrace' and rubbing shoulders with a crumbling methodist chapel of the same title, 'Primitive Methodists'. They were 'condemned cottages' alongside the ruin of the mill they once served, and designated slums, to be demolished, until the war gave them an extended life. For a period of time they had housed evacuees from the cities of Liverpool and Manchester when the bombing caused the unfortunate to abandon their shattered homes.

The village itself was Crawshawbooth, of little consequence to the reader I feel sure; but to a pair of newlyweds any town, large or small, clean or dirty will hold a tremendous impact on their future. And this was ours. It came about, not by choice, but necessity; a case of 'any port in a storm'. For weeks before the wedding bells were chiming, I had scoured the environs of Manchester for a future home. All to no avail. To that area I knew one day I would be working and would have to move, but for now, where indeed could we find a roof over our heads?

Then from high on the windswept road to Rochdale came an offer. Close to the bleak 'Owd Betts' inn stand a row of six quarrymen's cottages, at that time all minus the luxuries of running water, electricity or even gas. Lighting was by paraffin oil, or if unattainable, due to wartime restrictions, then by candle, and the water supply came from a hand operated pump to the rear of the block. Toilet facilities were early Victorian. All this anyway, was available at the acceptable figure of half a crown a week, so I jumped at the offer.

Indeed, I had all but paid an advanced rent when up came an even better proposition, and at only another shilling a week. Primitive Terrace was palatial in comparison; it even had gas lighting and an outside W.C. so to Crawshawbooth, and the two roomed dwelling we found ourselves on the night of the wedding.

With comparative ease the pair of us quickly adjusted to the lowering of the standards we were accustomed to in our previous homes. A case no doubt, of love being blind to inconvenience.

There would be no such thing as a honeymoon. Those things did not happen in wartime. I manoeuvred one day off, and that was to be utilised behind trowel and mortar board. The place hadn't been lived in for a year and after I'd spent half a day attempting to place two shillingsworth of plaster into a gaping hole in the lath and plaster ceiling, then picking it off the floor again, we started the main tasks; washing the walls and distempering them; wallpaper wouldn't be seen again for a few years yet. Covering the flagstone floor with 'utility' oilcloth, purchasing two pairs of curtains, two fireside chairs, a table and four chairs which took account of the entire allocation of coupons provided to a couple of newlyweds. Find a shop that would recharge the accumulators of the radio father had given me; that proved difficult so we went for the new service that Balls of Rawtenstall were providing ..... 'radio relay', with a choice of one station for one shilling a week, or two station, B.B.C. 'light' and 'home' services for one and sixpence.

What of the bikes..... Those cherished possessions could not stand outside. There was no place for a shed; the door opened straight out to the pavement and beyond that was the cinder roadway. They would have to take pride of place inside the room, and a sheet of newspaper was carefully laid over the shining new oilcloth; the china cabinet was relegated to a position in the far corner and a tandem and two solos wheeled in and ceremoniously placed against the window sill. Here they could drip oil and spread muddy lines across the folds of yesterday's newspaper and at the same time have utter protection from the ravages of inclement weather. It was all a priority of yesteryear, so funny in given retrospect.

I was proud of the three light gas chandelier. I hadn't realised they were

1, Group of *Hopkins Own,* 4th Rossendale scouts at Golborn camp in 1935. Author is seen centre of middle row flanked by Joe White and Billie Bates. Fred Rees bottom right and Norman Whitebread extreme top left.

2, An earlier group of *Hopkins Own* scouts off to camp about 1923. Note solid tyres on the lorry on the lorry and open sides.

3, Around the camp fires at *Fern Creek*. Douglas Taylor, Ron Bradshaw and Fred Rees. 1937

4, Hiking chums. Ron Bradshaw, Margorie Smethurst, Fred Rees and Sally Cook

5, Hostelling days. From left to right, Gladys Rees, Ron Bradshaw, Ron Booth Margorie Smethurst and Hilda.

6, An indomitable Quartet, Ron Bradshaw, Ron Booth, Laura Robinson and Dorothea Rees.

7, Twelve likely legs, and an unlikely refusal to hold the camera. A group of Rossendale Wheelers snapped by the author in 1949. Prominant and holding pipe in hand is Harry Evans who held the club together in the wartime years.
8, Just two of the 100 starters in the 1948 Richmond Road Race awaiting the starters flag. Seen here are the intrepid Jack (socks) Spencer, and Ron Bradshaw to the rear.

9, Tom Snape, crack 25 miler of immediate post war years and first to smash the hour record on Brock course. Seen here away to a fast start.

10, Ron Bradshaw with a furlong to go in the West Pennine Mountain time trial 1949.

11, Cyril Bradshaw under starters orders outside Rawenstall Town Hall when about to establish the out and home record to Blackpool in 1952. The holder is Johnny Kay, Timekeeper Jack Holden and alongside him wearing hat is Mayor of Rossendale, Alderman George Tomlinson.

Photo courtesy *Rossendale Free Press*

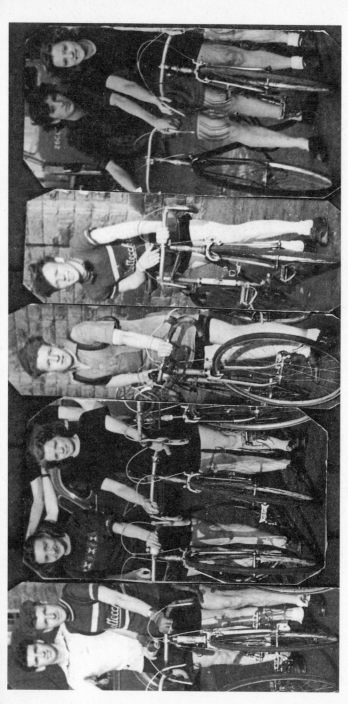

12, A composite picture of a few of the riders in the 1951 Festival of Britain Rossendale Time Trial - 25 miles. The course five laps of the circuit Rawtenstall - Waterfoot - Newchurch - Rawtestall. From left to right are: Peter Connolly, Ron Bradshaw, Marion Bradshaw, Dorothea Bradshaw, Cyril Bradshaw, Jack Bishop, Elizabeth Botterill and Doris Parkington.

Photo courtesy *Rossendale Free Press*

13, Ron Bradshaw climbing Mow Cop Hill in Staffordshire during the 1952 National Championships.

14, Eric Wilson, Rossendale Road Club. A true king of the hills. Four times National Champion. This picture taken in 1959. Photo courtesy *J. Love*.

manufactured until a friend gave me one. Even the gashes on the tubing all but disappeared after a good application of 'Brasso'. The gashes anyway were not my friend's fault. They were the result of the dreaded little 'yappers' that will appear charging from someone's front door to attack every innocent cyclist. This particular one I was ready for; at least twice a week on passing the Ashworth Arms he would charge from the corner, hell bent on bringing me to the ground and each time I had my pump in my right hand prepared for battle. A case of successive rapid swishes to left and right to stop him grabbing my foot or sticking his scrawny neck into my front spokes. But this time he had the last laugh, for the errant gas chandelier, swinging merrily from under my saddle made a direct attack on the back wheel; down I came, six spokes smashed, blood and skin embroidering the newly laid asphalt, and not a dog in sight..... though as I say, the brass chandelier was in near perfect condition.

Gas installation we quickly became accustomed to, there were not the likes of televisions and washing machines to operate at that time. It gave us the advantage of lighting, cooking, hot water, a gas poker to light the fire, and even a gas smoothing iron. But the one shilling slot meter we did NOT like; In particular when the shilling 'ran out' at some most inopportune moment. Like seven in the morning, when one partner jumped out of bed to find that very thing had happened, dressed in the dark but overlooked the fact that the tap under the light had been left open. The shilling subsequently tinkled down into the meter in the room below and there was light at the breakfast table, whilst upstairs there was NO light, only a stream of steadily hissing gas filling the bedroom. And the partner that had minutes before dived into the still warm bed following a night shift, all but 'snuffed it'.

Life in general, within our little community on 'Primitive Terrace' was an exercise in turning back the clock some thirty years. In any case, even then in the 'forties' there existed no materialistic priorities as those which haunt us today. No-one yet had heard of the term 'rat-race'.

Here I looked round at our proud little 'one room'. Bikes propped under the window, a massive kitchen range fireplace with oven to one side and water heater to the other, now ornamented with a huge cast iron kettle and a brass fender and iron stand. Each week there was the black leading and the 'Brassoing' to be done. Over in the corner at the top of the cellar steps stood the stone sink and a forlorn cold water tap, whilst above it the latest in gas technology, a hot water geyser.

We weren't without a bath either. When it wasn't in use, it stood down in the coal cellar! A battered old zinc vessel that leaked like a sieve. When it WAS in use you accomplished your ablutions in five minutes flat, or face sitting in this vacuous tub casting one eye at a shrivelled up big toe and the other a stream of soapy water cascading down the cellar steps. This happened to Dorothea the day she forgot to drop the catch on the door lock. Standing up there in her 'birthday suit' surveying the water as it careered under the dining table, whilst the front door shot open and in stepped the gas man to read the meter! No-one knocked before entering in our town.

There were even few inhibitions when you nipped off to 'spend a penny'. The toilet block was at the end of the street. No doubt an afterthought in the mind of some cotton baron many years after the houses had been built. There were two families allocated the use of one toilet, so often you waited your turn in the pouring rain, and carried on a mute conversation with the occupant who never seemed to be in any great hurry. Even through the paper thin walls the news of the day or topics mutual could be discussed. Sitting comfortably one day, Nancy Finney, our next door neighbour related her anecdote of the week. She had returned only yesterday from a week's holiday in Blackpool. The penultimate day had been wet and windy so the family took a coach trip to pass the day. It was a 'mystery tour', and the driver, eager to explore the hidden delights of industrial Lancashire had brought the party down this actual road, where from the confines of her seated luxury, she could distinguish clearly the chimney pot of her very own house!

I suppose that having no garden wall to lean over for a chat, this concourse was a comfortable alternative, although we did have the wall of the houses to lean against. That was providing you were careful not to inadvertently put your foot on the 'coal 'ole'. This was a metal cover protecting the shute, in turn a narrow cavity giving access to the coal cellar. It could be loose, and the journey down this black dust lined aperture held no glamour in the least.

I've had it to accomplish a few times. On the days when you lock yourself out and find it the better alternative to smashing a window or breaking down the door. At least there was a way through to the upstairs. Indeed our other neighbour, a gentleman who was both deaf and dumb had done likewise only last week. The snag was, he lifted the wrong cover in the dark of a winter's evening, slid down feet first into the murky depths and surfaced with a blackened face two minutes later in the wrong house..... OURS!

Though not very large, the cellar had other uses than storing coal. Apart from its convenience when moving to next door some months later, and knocking out a few stones to enable us to throw the remaining coal through, it proved large enough to house a small work bench.

Sited under a flickering gas mantle this innovation saw me putting a whole flight of old signal box steps to good use. They would make an admirable kennel for our latest guest, 'Snip'.

Our faithful friend of camping days was never far away. Living back in the valley again, he thought little of padding the four miles from Waterfoot and staying along with us for a few days. Not even a suitcase did he need to pack, but the house was not very large, and I considered he may appreciate a good sound kennel. That was when I got to work.

A week later, I stood back and proudly surveyed the finished product. Sturdy and solid; quite big enough too, he was no puny a hound, sufficiently wide to allow him to lie in comfort and tall enough for him to stand. It looked a master piece; and I'd been so scrupulous in my measuring of it, and I turned to haul it up the steps..... then I stopped dead. I hadn't measured the width of the steps: and there was a wall on either side!

In a rage of disgust my saw went straight down the middle, I carted it out and bought half a dozen bolts and fastened the thing together again. And to finalise my humiliation, Snip took an instant dislike to a kennel anyway, and dragged it half way down the street fastened to the end of his six foot chain, until the chain itself snapped in half.

We were very much attached to Snip. His rightful owner Dougy was away in the marines and Snip considered it a quite normal practice to travel periodically from one 'old friend' to another.

Destined as he was to be a roamer, he had always been in the company of our little gang of lads in Waterfoot. He had hiked alongside us over Pennine paths and moors in any and every direction; camped with us regularly on all our various sites on the Rooley Moors and in the Yorkshire Dales. To follow four young cyclists pedalling furiously in order to 'drop him' as far afield as Clitheroe, Preston, Burnley or Rochdale gave him no problem at all; he revelled in it. When we arrived back at night, there he was, eagerly waiting to greet us. His sense of direction was phenomenal.

Now, after an absence of several years, I had returned, and he had found a long lost friend. I had found my way back to Rossendale Valley. So whilst his master Douglas was away in the Royal Marines, and his other adopted master Fred Rees was in Ceylon, he would settle in with me. Sometimes arriving at work for the late shift I found him laying outside on the signal box steps. He would spend nine hours with me, and later calmly wander back to Waterfoot at eleven o'clock whilst I cycled home in the opposite direction.

Several times in later years, I would receive messages from various boxes on the line between Stubbins and Bacup, "Ron, your dog's here", the usual reply was "Don't worry, send him off and he'll find me", and surely he did before the day was out.

Not long after the demise of Snip's kennel, and the batterings it had taken on the wall of our cellar steps, I was surveying the damage to the wall itself. That was little, due to the fact that no plaster existed and the bare stone was merely a division between the back to back houses. Perhaps we could have a drop down table here, at the top of the steps suggested Dorothea, it would be so very useful alongside the sink and tucked away in the corner. Yes, said Ron, he would fix it. Why not?

But I am not in any way gifted when it comes to the finer points of joinery. Give me a hammer and a saw, and some form of pleasure will result in the chain of consequent destruction. So it proved on that fateful day.

It was a time before the refinement of the electric drill and the made to measure wall plugs had arrived in the ironmongers' shops. The big hammer, and a one foot stone chisel were my tools, and a six inch wedged shaped piece of timber would plug the wall in order to finish off the job. That was after I'd put together a reasonably square table top and swinging bracket. So now came the time to chisel between the stone work. It was work I enjoyed and treated with gusto. A six inch hole should be ample, and I slammed away viciously at that hunk of tempered steel. It became monotonous, nevertheless the chisel sunk deeper and deeper; and then, with the penultimate swipe having been carefully calculated the very worst happened. A six inch hole in a five inch thick wall spells disaster, and the roving chisel echoed its arrival on 'next door's' stone staircase, with a resounding thud.

This devastated handyman bent down and peeped through the hole. Mrs. Cannon was expressing the same surprise as me, and she was distinctly not amused. She stood in front of a mirror half naked, and a comb in her right hand that seemed to have frozen in mid air. It only made matters worse when I blew the dust through and called out an apology. Up to that point, we had been friendly neighbours.

In the evening I went round to see her husband, primarily to offer to repair the damage and secondly to recover my chisel. He was a comparatively close friend but seemed to suddenly have distanced himself, and

anyway, he got the last laugh. Six months later he moved out and we took over
his house; complete with the patched up hole in the wall, and an unintentional
two tone decor.

In all, the year of 1945 was extremely kind to us; as indeed to millions
the world over. It spelt the end of the war. May in Europe, and August
in the Far East. Dorothea's pregnancy, in its early stages curtailed
cycling activities though we did find time for a belated honeymoon, and
chose walking as the suitable alternative.

Almost every road throughout the Lake District had passed under our
wheel by now, and all the high peaks have beckoned. Only boots and a
rucksack could take you to the summit of Gable, Scafell or Pillar
mountain..... So the choice of venue was Stool End Farm at the head of
Great Langdale, and the season early spring; the month of March when
flash snowstorms or an unpredicted gale catch out the unwary.

Hardly a better centre could come our way for the exploration of the
central fells; That is Bow Fell, the Langdale Pikes, Esk Hause, Lingmell,
Great Gable, and England's highest, Scafell Pike at over 3,000 feet; all
are so easily accessible.

It proved a superbly gratifying week, with lashings of home cured bacon
and real farm butter spread across the breakfast table; boiled ham and
steaks in place of Spam and powdered eggs. Treats long forgotten in a
land of ration books and queues at the butchers.

As regards the hiking, things were kept in proportion. Carrying an unborn
child across this terrain is not everyone's choice of pre natal therapy, but
there were moments of apprehension no less. An hour spent on the
summit of Scafell when a sudden snow storm pinned us to the stones of
the cairn for shelter; and seeking the hair raising descent over a sea of
white dusted boulders. Or the day the heel collapsed on Dorothea's boot
whilst descending the evil 'slabs' on Bowfell..... You could hardly be expected
to carry a last, hammer and nails on a day's fell walking. But a tin opener,
a penknife and a couple of stones can work wonders.

A wonderful day arrived. It was midsummer and Dorothea gave birth to a
baby boy. We christened him Frederick. The days were all magic. V.E. day
had come and gone. The V.J. night; celebrations non ending in an austere
Britain, but nobody cared. In time all would return to normal. By next year
conscripts would return again, those that still lived that was. And things
would be the same again..... but they never were!

Came the year later. It was a cold January day when all our laughter turned to tears. There was no cure then. The little mite writhed in convulsion; it was double pneumonia and he died an hour after we watched his first struggles.

The shock was profound. We buried him twix our school and the church. In a hillside grave where the winds of time would heal the wound.

CHAPTER 10

RACING SADDLES

Spring brought the sunshine. It cleared the clouds and gave us new light. Our path was clear, only the call of the outdoor would ease the pangs of sorrow. Cumbria was calling again.

Then, as now; if ever we seek solace, it is to the fern and bracken of a mountain ghyll we hasten. In seven wonderful days, without ever a trace of rain or foul weather, six hostels passed our way as we tramped the mountain tracks from the shores of Wastwater to the heights of Helvelyn and Skidaw. On return it was back in the saddle once more. Our pals were returning in succession and their love of the open road had not diminished.

Inevitably, it would be Mrs. Mellors at Worston where we would all meet up in those post war years. For North Lancs cyclists it was a mecca, though however she made her establishment pay I fail to understand. There you would find all of forty bikes stacked up against her walls whilst every rider would have piled inside with a bagful of sandwiches and be gorging himself and drinking endless cups of tea from huge enamel tea pots. If you wanted to meet a crowd or an individual you knew, then it was to Mrs. Mellors you came.

It could be a Burnley club, or one from Bolton, Todmorden, Blackburn or Rochdale; the likes of Denis Ascough, Brenda Greenhalgh, Harry Benson and his sister Eva. Perhaps an odd member of the Rossendale Wheelers, a club that all but faded in the war years.

All the hostels, a few years previously high on the list of favourites were back in the itinerary of the faithful. Ingleton in particular. We never arrived at this hostel to be turned away saying it was full. Full it could well be, but the warden never did say that. He appeared to know just about everyone in the village and a bed was always available for the traveller. Over a period of time too, I believe we have slept on the floor of every school room and church hall in the place. The chip shop close to the hostel here must have fared well from the onslaught of many a cyclist arriving in the village with a 'knock on'. I recall once stopping outside this establishment with barely the energy to pull on a brake lever and crawling up to the counter to demand a shillingsworth of chips; five times the customary 'two pennath', and downing the lot myself.

We were a happy team that rode the highways and byways of the north that year. Fred was back and with Nora, now his wife, to make a new tandem team; my brother Cyril, on safe ground again after clearing beaches with the bomb disposal squad, was a new member of the team; Dougy had returned home and he too donned his shorts and cycling shoes once more. With Eva Benson often riding with us between her varied interests of walking and even racing, the group of us were a happy and carefree unit.

It was sad then, when not a great deal later we were to hear of Eva's tragic accident on the slopes of Snowden in North Wales. She had slipped on the notorious Crib Goch climb and was tragically killed. In her memory the West Pennine Road Club of Bury donated a cup, to be raced for annually in the clubs 'Ladies 25', a time trial held on Brock course in North Lancs.

At this time a tour of Devon and Cornwall was at the back of our minds. My leave this year, now extended to a fortnight would be in October and a thrust to the south appeared the most sensible suggestion. But what of my ancient steed, my contemporaries all seemed to be astride the latest models whilst I still pounded away on a self assembled A.S.P.!..... One answer to that spoke Dorothea in appropriate wisdom..... 'stop smoking!''

With that, I did. A promise to abstain for a period of twelve months passed my lips, and I held to it. Twenty five pounds was the cost of the 'Hill Special', I had in mind and twenty six pounds was the total cost of what went up in smoke over fifty two choking weeks.

So it came about. A time to 'ink in' the long line from South Wales to Lands End, and along the South Coast to Exeter, and be well on the way to completion of the 'End to End' dream.

Fourteen more hostels would round up a total of one hundred and twenty two visited to date, and the journey ahead proved one more success in a chain of two wheeled adventures.

Initially, the train to South Wales, then a visit to Chepstow and a crossing of the Severn on the old ferry boat. Bristol and Bath, Wells and Minehead. Porlock Hill in Somerset to Countesbury Hill in Devon. Then Clovelly in Cornwall and almost every cove to the delights of St. Ives and on to the windswept tip of the south west corner of England.

In every way it had been a success. The evocative sounds of a high wind in Mevagissy, or the rotting timbers of a wharf to be seen where once sailing ships tied up in Falmouth. Or the golden sands of a deserted beach on the south coast of Devon. Long before the motor car came to spill its teeming thousands, and to fill the air with 'beat' and 'punk'. We crossed the Tamar and rode through a blitz torn Plymouth, the skeleton of a city, and on to the placid waters of the Dart and ultimately to Exeter, to board the nigh train home.

A brief spell of hostelling followed this particular tour but it was to prove our last. At the close of this indelible phase I looked back; were there any two hostels alike? It is doubtful, all were so wonderfully individual, their character, their company and doubtless an important fact, their wardens.

It had been six years of nostalgic companionship, not only with your immediate pals but with the hundreds of wayfarers who traversed the country not only seeking a cheap night's accommodation, but a companionship that has sadly passed away with the course of time. The simple style, and the self made entertainment is a ghost of the past, the hostel of today, a shadow.

Cycle racing, in any of its competitive forms, velodrome or open road, was a sport that hitherto had generated little appeal to myself. The rough and tumble of any other outdoor athletics I shied a little away from. Even at school when they were picking the football team for some dreaded contest, I would be the first volunteer for a linesman's duties, and reading through 'Cycling' each week the racing pages were quickly flipped through as I searched eagerly for the articles of G.H.S., and any other topic of touring interest.

Considering, in the broad sense, there is little to equate the sport of cycle racing, and the pastime of touring. Each has its own place; as one who would view the comparison to driving a motor car with the family for a picnic on the downs, to hurtling round Silverstone in a formula two Ferrarri, or to having a dip in the sea at Blackpool, to entering the 500 metres freestyle at the Olympic Games. Each has its place.

So when one member of our tight little band, who shall remain nameless, proposed that he and I, hard riders and known stalwarts of the saddle could make a vivid impression in the field of cycle racing I was not over enamoured. But, try anything once, I usually would.

I gazed apprehensively at my skinny legs. Yes, they could do with a course of 'toning up'. I was doubtful I would have ever won even a 'knobbly knees' contest; so thin was I at the time; should I have faced the judge sideways he would have failed to see me at all! Over a period of time successive efforts to right the wrong have been tackled.

Chest expanders faced an untimely death; I struggled so hard to stretch the coiled springs across my puny chest that when the bands finally twanged back, they ripped out the only two hairs that had ever succeeded to gain a footing.

Thereby he scored his point. I would acquiesce. Plans were laid, and we went down to the sports shop for a bottle of 'Ellimans'. If you were to be 'one of them', you couldn't go anywhere without this potent reliever of all muscular pain.

Instinctively, there was no other better man to go to for advice on the next procedures than the fabled Jack 'socks' Spencer. 'Socks', as he was affectionately known had been born in the saddle all were adamant; he certainly died in the saddle after a lifetime's devotion to the sport many years later. At this point he was managing the Rawtenstall shop of C.H. Parsons.

In pre war years, about the time that Parsons severed his connections with Greenwood in Waterfoot, 'Socks' was a dominant rider with the Rossendale Wheelers, but along with a faction of the more competitive minded, broke away to form the Rossendale Road Club. The latter club had disintegrated when war broke out, but now the indomitable Jack Spencer was back; and back to make an impact.

Should I be asked to nominate three racing cyclists who produced a maximum, in their efforts to publicise cycling sport in the Rossendale Valley, then Jack Spencer, Johnny Palmer and Eric Wilson must surely deserve the highest accolade.

Palmer, a post war master of long distance riding, had, for a few magical moments held the 100 miles national time trial record in the late thirties, whilst Wilson in more modern times, and a man of totally different calibre took undisputed supremacy in the hills, becoming four times British hill climbing champion.

Jack Spencer however, was a perpetual all rounder, in every meaning of the word. He won races from 1939 until 1979, then met a tragic death, still doing what he liked above all else; riding a bike. If gales lashed the Brock course in North Lancs, he would win a '50' or a '25'; if snow or sleet barred the way in an early season training event, he would crash his way through and cross the line first. When he regained consciousness after a multitude of crashes he would ever be laughing. Superbly at his best under the cruellest of conditions.

He must be our obvious mentor, and to him we presented ourselves one bitter day in the month of February 1947. Jack had all the answers; first we would be recruited into the West Pennine Road Club, a constellation renowned in the field of racing. And as it happened also, a club that now recruited members we knew well of old. The likes of Harry Benson, who would go on to become a 12 hour rider of repute, Henry Richardson and Denis Ascough, two likely comedians of dry wit, and Jimmy Revell, the lad that forever turned up at some hostel or other having conveniently forgotten his sandwiches, and cadging one from each of the assembled group, thereby finishing up with twice the amount of food as anyone else! Next in the process of instruction, or possibly ELIMINATION, came the 'training run'. A loose term that could mean, you had won the mock 'race', been seen somewhere along the road, or that you would never be seen again..... We made it; just about!

The new 'Hill Special' and the brand new 'Hobbs of Barbican' were shining like new pins as we awaited the promised bunch of athletes. Great expectation we held, having been told to leave behind mudguards, saddlebags and any excess weight, then at the appointed time of nine o'clock they arrived; TWO only that was. None other than 'Socks' himself, and the now legendary Tom Snape, fastest man north of the city, where only Cyril Cartwright held greater honours.

We were devastated; it was a bitterly cold morning, a legacy of the infamous winter of that decade; and here we were, two complete racing novices about to be chaperoned by two of the fastest men in the north of England.

"Just tuck in at the back" hissed Tom Snape;. He was a quiet man! "If you get dropped we'll hole up for you in Settle." At that point we were in Bury, some fifty miles south. I think Tom that very morning was setting his sights on the day a year or two ahead when he would become the first man in the north to beat the magic 'hour' for a 25 mile time trial, and be only the fourth man in the country to have accomplished that feat at that time.

We were off at a devastating pace. By the time we passed Whalley the ground had been covered in half the time we were used to. My lungs were bursting and I expected my calf muscles to seize up at any second. Having seen nothing but the wide protection of Jack's broad back and behind, I felt sure they must be tiring as the sharp steep hill outside Rathmall approached. WE always 'walked' that one. But none of it; one second they were here, then they were gone; like the greyhound from a racecourse trap!..... In all respect, it must be recorded, they kept their promise and waited in Settle.

A lot we had learned; but again, there would be a lot more. That particular

hill was known as a 'prime', one of many chosen on a road race course where
auxiliary prizes are awarded the first man over the line.

Fixed wheels and a 69 inch gear were the order of the day for training,
there wasn't even any rest downhill; and to walk up a hill was unheard
of. Had you have succumbed to that indignity, then you would be well
advised not to show your face in the clubroom for a period of a month
at the very least.

We were learning fast, two more of these epic feats of endurance and I
returned home to collapse trembling into a chair and gaze down at my
prostrated legs; I didn;t really think they were still there. But, yes, they
weren't just straight anymore; they had little mounds both on the thighs
and the calf. It MUST be muscle. I sat that evening engrossed in the 'Cycling',
reading those words of graphic encouragement from the pen of an unchallengeable
racing columnist, Harry Aspden. Had I not succumbed to his colourful yarns
depicting the exploits and endurances of the great Gino Bartalli, and his
contemporary challenger and countryman, Fausto Coppi, I think at that stage,
I may not have gone any further. Though loathe to admit it at the time, I was
hooked.

Our racing secretary, Johnny Potter, was the embodiment of efficiency;
before we had chance to think otherwise, he had the fees from us and with
little choice in the matter, we were entered for a 'longmarkers', or
novices "25", to be held on the Monks Heath course in north Cheshire.
The day came and it was appalling. It lashed with ice laden rain from start
to finish, the wind did its very best, determined to smash the hopes of any
budding Reg Harris or Basil Francis. But in the end, shivering and
dripping gallons of rainwater from a soddened black jersey and shorts,
the pair of us staggered to the timekeeper's assistant, disenchantedly
writing up the finishing times.

Even in that state I could have jumped for joy; done a jig, or whatever;
we had both cracked it. Nowhere near winning the event itself, having a
hundred entrants, but recording times of under one hour fifteen minutes;
the magic 'evens', twenty mile an hour for twenty five miles and at a speed
that any potential racing man must achieve on his first venture if he is to show
any hope of progression.

I was sad that my companion never raced again, yet for me the die was
cast. For the foreseeable future, there was a new life calling, and 'riding
a bike', would never be the same again.

Embarking upon a career, or merely the pastime of cycle racing means,

I quickly discovered the complete reappraisal of simply sitting on a bike; let along the rhythm of controlled breathing, and correct handlebar position. There is the matter of smooth ankle action to gain every ounce of pressure, and saddle height, which, as often is the case, displays the inexperienced rider far too high or forward over the bracket. Toe clips, straps, and blocks on racing shoes all play their part, and comfort, in addition to speed is of prime importance. There won't be time to stop and readjust a saddle that's attempting to shave off every inch of burning skin from your crotch in the middle of a 50 mile race! And it must be remembered that there is a world of difference in the construction of a bike that is intended to win a 400 metre sprint on the track, and that of the road bike that's expected to take its rider some 250 miles in a 12 hour time trial.

Inspired by the convictions of 'Socks' that one day I would 'make it', the early training of the season brought its promised results. By late summer bronze medals came my way for the time trial distances of 25, 50 and 100 miles; the highlights having been a 'handicap' win in the Pyramid Road Club 100 mile race, and a Lancashire Road Club medal for topping over 200 miles in the first attempt at a 12 hour trial. Later, to add fire to my enthusiasm the club's cup for the best novice of the year was awaiting me at the annual dinner and prize presentation.

The 'off season' festivities were a revelation to me. It was alien to my concept of cycling's winter activities. Hitherto, the common room of some distant hostel garlanded in snow or fog had been a venue for winter gatherings. But then again, I was among a different breed of rider; these were the athletes; the ones who let off steam when the rigid demands were unshackled, and who was I to argue.

Frank Hudson was the tower of strength that drove a virile club to its successes, in both the racing and the social sphere. A pillar of inspiration to all the racing fraternity, and a brilliant organiser when the needs of winter's socialising came around.

The Derby Hall, across the square from Robert Peel's monument, and now demolished was the venue for the West Pennine annual 'do' in Bury, and as with all others, the fraternity came from far and wide. Likewise, we all reciprocated. There were weekends at Blackpool for the Flyde Road Club's occasion, Bolton for the Lancashire Road Clubs, or Blackburn for the north Lancs Clarion, even as far as York where Tom Snape had some shield, or cup to be awarded.

This was a great time for abstention from the rigours of strict training and competition, in place a few pints of ale passed our lips, but it mattered little. Those would be sweated out when the last day of February dawned.

And when it did dawn there was elation. No-one was completely unfit. There was always an element of 'secret' exercise in the winter. I alone knocked up some 150 miles a week riding to work and back alone. Well could I be plodding home bleary eyed after a night shift and spot some member of a local club out 'getting in' a few crafty miles before going off to work. And then there were those 'rollers' for training in the clubroom.

The first 'loosener' of the season then would likely be a forage into the hills of Bowland, with Jack Spencer in the lead endeavouring hard to shake off a stone of his excess weight. Leaving Bury at nine in the morning it would become a veritable massed start road race with Lancaster the target for lunch, and the wilds of Tatam Fell as a prologue. If you had time, you may have had the inclination to raise your head and catch a fleeting glance of the Ashton Memorial, presiding in Victorian majesty across the Bay of Morecambe. That in effect would have been doubtful, in all probability, 'Socks' just getting his second wind, would be calling back to crash on to Nicolson's at Brock; they made a better pot of tea there!

Another factor in all this challenge for road supremacy among the racing clubs, stemmed in a very large way from the advent of the Olympic Games the coming year. The fact that they were to be held in Britain added impetus to national interest and even the press, lukewarm in their coverage of matters cycling were awakening to the fact that in Reg Harris, national sprint racing cyclist he alone carried the probability of Gold Medal acclaim for our country. In Harris, and Cyril Cartwright, we had strong contenders on the track, but the composition of a road racing team was as yet wide open. George Flemming from the south, Maitland and Bowes from the Midlands and 'tiny' Thomas from Yorkshire were already high in the minds of the selectors, though it had been announced that one hundred 'possibles' were to be chosen early in the coming year, and from now on, the challenge to prove your potential at least, was the criterion. Looking back, to have had the rare chance to be chosen even to ride in a selection event, is now my cherished memory.

With scant consideration for time and trouble we would ride endless miles in the search for racing equipment. These were yet days of accepted austerity following our country's unmitigated war effort. If Ossy Jackson didn't have what you wanted in Nelson, then off you tore to Ron Kitchen's in Harrogate. It could be a Simplex gear, and 'Alex' racing jersey or shorts, perhaps a pair of 'Sherens' racing shoes. A round trip of 120 miles mattered little, and was no deterrent; it was all put down to another training run.

Inspiration was never lacking among the riders of the day. Tragically, the chances to race on the open road were. In Britain this was not possible owing to legislation at the time, and diehards of the old school who kept us to time trials and secrecy. Shivering before the likes of Sam Williams or Frank Slemen with their regulation watches at six in the morning, away from all civilisation on some flat expanse of open road in the Flyde or Merseyside.

In the Isle of Man, the only place in Great Britain where public roads were closed for sport, we watched that year in humiliation as the Frenchman Jean Baldasari and his team raced over the line to take a first, second and third placing, leaving the cream of British cycling struggling in the rear. In the game of massed start road racing we had a lot to learn indeed. Notably, it came to almost a decade before a British rider was to even FINISH in the epic 'Tour de France'. Brian Robinson took that honour in the mid fifties after winning the British hillclimbing championship and turning professional.

In such a lamentable situation, where little or no chance to involve yourself in the branch of the sport that appeals most is offered, then one must turn again to the closest alternative, which is time trialing. There are always personal best times to be bettered, even if there is little likelihood of actually winning the event. That is the overall attraction of riding against the clock, and a further incentive, to know you have done it entirely on your own, without help from any other competitor or even a favourable wind, you both start and finish at the very same spot.

With that in mind, and a past allegiance to the hard rider's dictum, the prospect of the 12 hour trial was paramount in my mind as the midsummer approached. To me, priding myself as somewhat an endurance rider, it was the ultimate.

It proved to be a revelation. Riding against the clock over a set time, as opposed to massing a substantial mileage during a carefree tour contrasted enormously. There were assets of course. At that time, before the likes of Stan Haslem and Ken Joy rode non stop to smash existing records, there were feeding stations where you stopped and took a quick bite, and hopefully didn't writhe along the ground in an agonising bout of cramp. It was at one of these, after six hours of continuous pedalling..... in those days it was the done thing to ride 'fixed gear'..... I 'died'. Twenty minutes I lay on the grass in untold bliss, until a friendly marshal eased me over with the toe of his shoe; ''You might as well ride on laddie and finish the course; you've got to ride back anyway." He was right, we were at Grange-over-Sands on the north side of Morecambe Bay and the finishing circuits were on the windswept Pilling Sands way down towards Blackpool.

So I 'toileted'; that helped. I eased an aching thigh over the cross bar with the help of a young female helper; that helped as well. And pulled away with fresh hope in the direction the marshal pointed, thankfully towards the finish.....

Then as the waters of the estuary alongside shallowed towards the Arnside Sands, the tide turned for me as well; it was the elusive second wind, today a little late blowing my way.

There were riders in front; I was catching and passing them. And in an orgy of self punishment the bike returned to life. Passing the 'drinks' area, that fleeting sanctuary where they run alongside and hand you up an aluminium bottle a little to the north of Carnforth, I felt I could ride on forever. It's then you snatch the bottle, little caring what's inside it; if it's orange juice and you tipped it over your head, that's too bad; if it was from a club mate and it had brandy in it that's even worse. The best solution is half over your head and the rest down your throat, and head down to the task again.

In any event, I claimed a bronze medal at the finish, and went on a year later to make it a silver, having learned a great deal more in the intervening months.

Riders today are more likely to appear at the start of an event such as these having just climbed from a car, their bike suitably shod in its racing tyres, and ready for the word go. Not so at that time. In all probability you would have ridden ten miles from your 'digs' to the start of the race, and after you had thrashed yourself for an average of 215 miles, would face a thirty mile ride home. Add the agony of the hills surrounding Rossendale and you would be ready to tackle sausage, egg and chips three times over when you staggered through the door close to midnight, as I myself could verify following three of these exploits.

Because the desire to improve one's performance was so deeply embedded, I sometimes look back in sheer amazement at some of the feats of endurance we suffered to attain only that aim. Take my wife, Dorothea. She was never a racing fanatic, yet I recall the day she and Doris Parkington set out to ride down to Derby to compete the following day in a ladies 10 mile event. It was not that either had the least chance of winning. Particularly when the vivacious Susie Rimmington was heading the list of entrants. No, it was simply to knock a few seconds off their best times, or at the best, a minute. Both of them left, as so many of us did, with their two cane rimmed racing wheels strapped to brackets alongside the front wheel, tubular tyres folded across their backs, to face a 200 mile return journey across Manchester the hills of the Peak District and a venue far away in Long Eaton. That was sheer enthusiasm; a total dedication to amateur sport. And then we picked up our newspapers to read of the nursing and pampering; the worship and the national fame of the continental riders to whom our country's contenders would next year be pitted against.

CHAPTER 11

OLYMPIC SADDLES

By and large, the promotion of the Olympic Games in Great Britain 1948 was grossly lacking the impact that we today would expect approaching the year 2000. The country had hardly shaken off wartime austerity, and yet, there were some forms of rationing. The razzamatazz of modern showmanship had not crossed the Atlantic, and television was available only to a fortunate few in the area of our capital city. As had been the norm over the past three decades we would read the newspapers, glue our ears to the radio, or pop down to the 'pictures' and glimpse a five minute summary on the newsreel, half way between the supporting and the main feature.

But the newspapers were kind to we cyclists in one respect. At least they were pointing to the fact that Reg Harris was likely to be our sole gold medal winner. The fact that he didn't in the end holds no disrespect to Reg; the result of that final heat was contentious at the time, and forever will be, and at least, he was amateur champion of the world and went on to become professional sprint champion for several years to come.

Roadmen were a different species however. They had to train and to race on the open, and often windswept roads outside of the towns; not for them the sheltered confines of a city velodrome. And a rain lashed course was no exception in the early months of this particular year.

Several events had been earmarked by the appropriate committee in order to wittle down one hundred Olympic possibles to a dozen probables and finally to the four who would line up with the world's best in the road race championship. In our locality, the two races that were to determine the fate of the West Pennine riders, were a 100 kilometre time trial in the hilly region of Ruthin and Llangollen in North Wales, and a more appropriate massed start road race on the closed circuit of Catterick army camp at Richmond in Yorkshire.

The two events were held in totally contrasting conditions. Whilst the mountain time trial over the Clywedian hills was marred by torrential and freezing rain, the race more akin to what was to be expected was fought under a burning sun and with all the publicity expected of a major gathering of notable athletes.

In consequence to the results of these, and several other events, the club was proud to see Tom Snape and Jack Spencer got forward to the list of probables and be ultimately placed on the reserve list. That in itself was a tribute to their prowess.

As for myself, I went the way of a thousand other hopefuls. Yet to have had the honour of at least a place in the chosen participants, was in itself a distinction. Something to cherish, until the final wave of a finisher's chequered flag.

To end notes on the dismal outcome of British participation in the games, I see standing piteously exposed the governmental inadequacies in coping with the requirements of international road racing. The sad tale of the Olympic Road Race fiasco in Windsor Great Park can be left to posterity.

At least to the country's racing bodies, the N.C.U. and the R.T.T.C. the message had been spelt out loud and clear. There was need for open road massed start racing, and time trials far from the fastest courses available. To where the all rounder could show his talent, and where mountain passes would oft determine the course of combat. Hadn't Pellisier, Maes, Bartalli and now Fausto Coppi shown the world a mastery of the humble cycle. Legendary, the name of Coppi at that time drew an aura of invincibility; a superman who was king of the mountains, a winner of the fabled Tour de France, the classic Milan-San Remo and the Paris-Roubaix, and had now smashed the world's one hour record on the board track in Milan. Never would feats of that nature have been possible by simply riding against the clock at six in the morning on some flat, dull and uninteresting road way out on the plain of York.

There was a reluctance on the part of the diehards, but inevitably it came. One of the first races to herald the change, and I am proud of the fact, was the West Pennine Mountain Time Trial. Held over two laps of the Holcombe course, in subsequent years it was to become an open road race in the true sense. Locally too, came the N.L.T.T.A. trial through the hills of Bowland, and the Tour of the Dales, fifty miles of hill and dale around the now legendary Settle to Carlisle railway line. Country I knew like the back of my hand; but had little time to stare at now.

This kind of racing I revelled in, and its pursuit found myself travelling as far as Northumberland, for the 'Tour of the Cheviot'. All these races found me with higher placings than ever I got on the flat, or the fast courses. From the elation that comes when you outclass a rider of repute on the slopes of a five mile climb, I knew then, that hill climbing was my one hidden asset. Time would prove this, but these were yet early days.

Despite the rigours of serious training, and the deadly serious stance at the start of a race, there is a lighter side. Instance the evening before one York Road Club 'Easter' 50 mile T.T. We Lancastrians rolled up to the Bay Horse Hotel in York, to find ourselves billeted alongside the Huddersfield Road Club, very much a pack of staunch defenders of the 'white' rose. Following the evening meal there seemed an air of anticipation, which began to manifest itself in the bar later in the evening. That was after the locals had disappeared to other hidden rooms and our two dozen combatants lined up the pints. What made matters worse was that Harry Benson, not riding on the morrow, was a twelve pint man, and Dougy Taylor who had come along as my 'helper' would be legless after only two, and could only stop when someone removed the barrel.

There hadn't been any gun fired but all knew it was to be a battle. A 'Roses' war, with ale as the ammunition. MY own problem however was not the beer. It was the wanton gaze of the barmaid whose name was Olga, and only afterwards I was to learn, she was not simply known as Olga, but "Olga, the vulgar barmaid", with no disrespect to the traditional Russian folk song. Even to this day the sordid detail of events that evening escapes me, in fact I very much doubt they were at all clear when Dougy tipped me out of bed at five in the morning to prepare for the 50 mile race at six. There are misty recollections of female underwear scattered around my immediate vicinity at the stoke of midnight, and of the landlord having gone off to bed and leaving the staunch Frank Hudson in charge of the bar.

Needless to say, I didn't win the race; not that I was expected to. I don't recall ever finishing. But if there were no cycling medals for upholding the honour of Lancashire, at least it seemed there was established a certain sense of concupiscent victory that would epitomise the land of the 'red rose', and follow me awesomely around the 'circuit' for many a year to come.

To the other side of the coin, forgetting the lighter side, must fall the unpredicted failures; the long journey to Surrey where you are listed as 'scratchman' in a middlemarkers '25' and puncture at the halfway mark. The same journey again five years later when you are confidently expected to claim the major award in a hill climb, and collecting a 'flat' 200 yards out. A broken chain in the first yards of a climb you've trained on for weeks, and now you'll wait another year for a second chance.

To the 'scratchman', the potential winner, and often the record breaker, the disappointments can be intense. On the East Lancs road the Pyramid Road Club 30 mile T.T. had become a classic, mainly because there were so few '30's' and in the late forties there were many men capable of smashing the national record. Jimmy Bell of Duckinfield Road Club was one of these; he happened to be one minute off behind me at the start, and the conditions that year were superb. A rising wind, not too strong was blowing from the west and on this course, with only traffic islands a hazard, records that morning were set to tumble.

At the 15 mile turn, Bell was on my tail. The fact that he had not already passed me had set my blood tingling; not expected in the least to take a prize in this event, our own club record was now a strong possibility, and the wind from the turn was now the greatest friend anyone could wish. We were alongside as Haydock Island approached, and the fact that Jimmy was not gaining gave me a frenzied recklessness. It was obvious neither was going to give way as we came in to the curve, and then the inevitable happened. The two of us leaned together, the surface glistened with an evil coat of treacherous oil and four wheels went under in the very same second.

By the time we had extracted ourselves from a tangle of buckled wheels and bent cranks, the loss of time, and blood into the bargain swept away any chance of remounting and returning a respectable time. Jimmy Bell lost his chance of the national record, and I bear a souvenir scar where the bone was bared, to this very day. And of the man that so bitterly lost his one chance to be the national record holder, he simply laughed out loud, jumped on his wheel rims until they turned in his forks, and hobbled back to race headquarters; I've never seen him since!

In view of a plea from the then secretary, and additionally due to the fact that I resided in Rawtenstall, I transferred my allegiance to the Rossendale Wheelers in mid '48, and became their secretary at the same time. It proved not a prudent move. Secretarial work and the added aggravations of night work and shift duties are not conducive to producing your best in the field of sport.

Nevertheless the club, not in the past having been racing orientated, had material such as Jim Jordon, Dave Cross, John Chapman, Marion Cain, John and Jean Murgatroyd and Jack Bishop, all waiting the chance to show their prowess. In due course the likes of Raymond Horsfall, Alf Tootill, Derick Ireland, Peter Connolly, Harry Pickup, Melvyn Tetlow and my brother Cyril, would swell the ranks. They were all extremely keen and in a very short time the nucleus of racing section to the club would be moulded. In an extremely short time they were notching up creditable times on the courses at Copster Green, Brock, and on the east Lancs. As for myself, the very day our second son was due for discharge from the maternity home, I clocked up my best '25' to date, thirty miles away.

So in due course, and irresistibly, the young bloods were making their mark. They were teenagers, and all but ten years my junior, and the urge to prove their par to an 'old' man of doubtless years of experience was paramount.

That rivalry, and a flair for competition gets the best from all. The club championship that year promised a close duel; and so it proved. In the end I took it, but only by a bare margin over the fast improving Jim Jordon.

And it was Jim, and Dave Cross that gave a tremendous challenge in the Wheelers annual Waterfoot to Blackpool time trial. An event long on the calendar of the Wheelers, and won at first by Johnny Palmer in pre war years. Usually won in a time of around one and a half hours, the C.H. Parsons trophy was all but mine to be taken outright in a third win, but I reckoned without the threat of an up and coming Alf Tootill.

The club championship, as with that of the national championship was decided on an average speed, recorded during the season in 'open' time trials over the distances of 25, 50 and 100 miles. I enjoyed this form of racing, but it was not a favourite, and as would come to light in successive years with the Rossendale Road Club, my best performances were in the hills. The long distance 12 hour trials too were a vocation. In all probability a throw back to long distance touring days. Who other in their right state of mind would contemplate a 205 mile training spin to Glasgow, throwing in Shapfell and Beatock, and into the teeth of a howling north west wind. Or a morning spin following a night shift to Holmfirth on the other side of the Pennines, merely for a try out on the five mile Holme Moss climb against the watch.

If not in the top class when it came to national competition, at least it seemed I had potential as a hill climber. And likewise, did several of my club companions. It was said by Harry Aspden at one club dinner speech, that the terrain Rossendale riders had to contend with bred a club of hill climbers, and how right his words proved to be in ensuing years.

The very first time my own innate ability flared was during the N.L.T.T.A. Mountain T.T. in Bowland Forest. A certain 'young blood' of the Flyde Road Club, a 'one hour man' on the flat L6 course was 'Off' one minute behind me, and with customary zest, caught, and passed me, within eight miles and along the flat early miles. That very fast start and his total lack of experience on a climb were his undoing. On the vicious one in four hill from Quernmoor to the high summit he was last seen struggling to even keep his balance, let alone finish the course. In the Trough of Bowland, I found a climbing rhythm that had me passing two more 'scratchmen' and at the finish gain a creditably high placing from the 120 starters. I believe it was the first time the pleasure of seeing my name in the first ten of an 'open' T.T. had come my way.

Doubtless it was this egotistic boost, and the plain fact that flat roads held no appeal whatsoever to me which led not only myself, but other keen members of the club to diversify, and shortly there were fresh grounds to challenge, if not to conquer.

A positive result to the diversification over subsequent years, were the successes both of myself and the club in the late season hill climbs. My own weight of a little over nine stones, an easy climbing style and systematic devotion to deep breathing exercises aided tremendously, and soon I was club champion in that field of the sport. Added to this came third, then second in the Lancashire championship, and other very high placings for both myself and the club team. If nothing else, it formed an inspiration, and I consider this the foundation of the many successes that would come the way of Rossendale cyclists in the very near future. Unknown to us few then, the future champion of Great Britain, though only a mere stripling of eight stones and sixteen years old was watching our antics on Turnpike Hill in Waterfoot.

Inescapably involved in the game of open road racing, as opposed to time trialling, no-one can fail to escape the magic of a Fausto Coppi sat 'on the tops', leading a struggling pack behind him on some notorious pass in the Alps. The sheer glory, the thrill. You want to be him. You sense the smooth breathing, the struggle to let no man know how even you yourself are suffering, and to hear the panting, and the heavy swish of their wheels in your ear, knowing full well how they are out of the saddle and all but dropped.

It happened for me only once, but I treasure it forever. Albeit it wasn't in the fabulous Alps, but on the Holcombe climb in the first open road massed start road race held by the West Pennine Road Club. Subsequently, I was swallowed by the pack on the drop to Helmshore, but whilst the dream lasted, it was pure heaven.

Late in the year of 1949. like many other railwaymen of the time, I had become disgruntled with pay and conditions, and when someone suggested working in the cycle trade, an occupation that ought well to suit me admirably, I considered. C. H. Parson had already offered me a manager's post and I had declined, but when assistant manager at the Rochdale branch of Pira Cycles was later suggested, I succumbed. It was another of life's little mistakes, but I treasure the experience, it even brought me in a part time job in later years when the money was ill needed.

From Rochdale and Bolton as assistant, to full management in Manchester, and back again to Rochdale the job progressed, and likewise the training miles; often forty miles a day, I considered that a bonus; that was until the day one of those friendly dogs ran out to greet me in determined enthusiasm as I descended Norden Hill at about forty miles an hour. I finished in Rochdale Infirmary, and he finished on the vet's table for a final job; three postmen with tattered trousers were also the evidence the policemen wanted.

The only perquisites and advantages to the position I found there, were, cash discounted bicycle spares, more social hours of employment, and the one chance to pick my own holiday week; that I chose to be the week our one and only daughter was born in late 1950. Then it was back to the railway, and the life of a signalman which forever would be the love of my life.

All seemed fine as 1951 rolled in. It was the year of the Festival of Britain and great things were happening in the racing world. Inextricably involved in administration, the opportunities to promote and publicise the game were immense and I endeavoured to take every opening. But alas, there was friction in a mixed club and the inevitable happened, just as it had once before; the Rossendale Road Club was reborn. It took one hour at a meeting in 28 Woodcroft Street, and fifteen hard core workers from the racing section of the Wheelers. It was a significant evening.

Sharing the enthusiasm, Jack Spencer returned to his old club, Johnny Palmer returned the renowned 'Rose Bowl', and all the clubs cups and shield rolled back in from ex members far and wide. The mayor gave us his backing and the council donated a 'Festival of Britain' Cup, with the proviso we organised a road race in the town as part of the celebrations. Johnny Kay, local cycle manufacturer gave us the use of a clubroom over his shop, and local tradesmen and character extraordinary Jack Harvey was recruited as president; he proved an excellent choice.

In all there was nothing to halt the club's rapid progress, or to impede the members determination to build a successful cycle racing unit. slowly it took the course we had dreamed of. There were rollers in the club room for winter training, weekly meetings and socials held in the same room;

the whole set up was quickly taking shape.

Overnight an impact was achieved, and the Rossendale Road Club became a force to be reckoned with in national racing. Jack Spencer, already a celebrity gave the club's name a boost, then with our placings in the Richmond Road Race in Yorkshire, we achieved an invitation to compete in the national championship, to be held in the Isle of Man.

Following our unqualified success at Richmond the performance in the Isle of Man was a mini disaster however. All the team had an element of bad luck, of which my own was the worst.

As the flag dropped one hundred of the country's best surged forward, every one intent on getting to the front of the bunch before the tortuous bends and narrow section loomed. It was the Mannin Veg, a shortened version of the international course, where more laps could give added spectacle to the watchers. Consequently, the dreaded Governor's Bridge came early in the race; the one where hundreds gather to see the blood spill, and among others mine they would shortly see. Tootill, Horsfall and Cross were well to the fore, I could see their brand new club colours bobbing in the kaleidoscope. Elbows out is the order of the game as the bunch close and the road narrows into the hairpin, and brake blocks are rubbing at the front and bikes are inches apart. That is the order when someone's front wheel rams your gear mechanism into the rear spokes, and down you come. Crashing to the grit strewn road and a succession of riders thud into your back.

It was an inglorious end. They led me into the first aid tent and patched the broken skin. But it was my new jersey, the one with the new club colours we were proudly sporting that made me cry. In tatters and crisscrossed with the oil of half a dozen filthy chains.

Not for the first time had a new jersey of mine suffered a similar fate. The West Pennine colours had been sliced unmercifully with a pair of scissors from the prostrate body of 'Twitters' Entwhistle four years previously whilst he lay unconscious at this very same spot.

This particular bridge held some sort of voodoo on Rossendale riders. Only two years ago, Jack Spencer had a severe argument with the wall here and lay unconscious in Douglas Hospital for the best part of two days.

It was becoming a habit. And no racing cyclist could possibly have had more head injuries than Spencer. But at least on that particular championship day for the reborn Rossendale Road Club, only myself succumbed to the infamous bridge. My team mates made it, but only one finished the race. One suffered gear trouble and the other punctures; we boarded the night crossing back to the mainland that evening a subdued quartet.

Like any other tale of woe however, there can be a bright finish. I'm sure the young lady was not a qualified nurse, merely a keen supporter from one of west Lancashire clubs seeking to offer solace to the wounded, and I certainly was in pain as the hard boards of the ships deck grated against a bandaged shoulder and a half skinned left arm. She was adamant in her desire to succour, and I felt little resistance as her lithe fingers massaged, and her whispered endearments promised immediate relief to a night of predicted agony. Someone found a ships blanket to cover us, and afterwards, I slept well.

The 'Festival' race, a 25 mile time trial over five laps of a course taking in Rawtenstall, Waterfoot and Newchurch was a tremendous success. A great pity it could not have been raced under full road racing conditions, but those were the regulations at the time. What did surprise the public in general nevertheless, was the ease and speed of that riders climbed the 'one in six' Turnpike Hill. Until then they had witnessed people with cycles simply pushing them up the hill. That indignity was unknown to the three riders shortly to become the team champions of Lancashire, and who climbed in style that day. And what was unknown even to them alone, that watching from a roadside vantage point, was a stripling of eight stones only, a lad that vowed one day he would climb that hill faster than any of those racers he watched. And sure enough, as time went by he did; and indeed, many more hills. He was destined to become champion of Great Britain. His name: Eric Wilson.

Gaining publicity too for the club at that time were the girls. Doris Parkington and her sister Edith, Dorothea Bradshaw, Jean Murgatroyd, Marion Caine and Elizabeth Botterill. All were now in the silver medal class and the club's prestige was growing by leaps and bounds.

We considered it high time we had a shot at track racing; perhaps merely to publicise the club, or to simply say we had done it. Our nearest cycle tracks were at Fallowfield in Manchester, twenty miles distant, or Bootle track in Liver[pool, thirty five miles from home. Not by any means an attractive proposition when considering a track bike, with fixed wheel and one brake only had to be ridden that distance first, before stripping the brake and preparing perhaps for a gruelling 4000 metres pursuit race. Nonetheless we would try it.

It was the only one time I met Reg Harris; world sprint champion at the very time. We didn't speak, firstly because he didn't know me, and secondly because he came by me on the steeply banked Fallowfield stadium at about twice the speed I myself was travelling. All this sort of thing happens when you are using the track for training, and HE is using you as pawn in the game of sprint finishing at forty miles an hour. I was accompanied by Raymond Horsfall who at the time, along with Tootill, and Tetlow were to compete in the North Lancs area team pursuit championships. The trouble was though, the area didn't have a cycle track under its own jurisdiction, and we were bundled off to Liverpool to ride the preliminary round. As it happened we got no further; a brilliant first lap by Tetlow who was then dropped did us no good at all, as a far superior track team from the Flyde crossed their line with ten seconds to spare.

A similar sad story found myself knocked out of the second round of the individual pursuit when drawn against the short distance wizard from Blackburn, a youthful Ken Hartley, again at the windswept Bootle track on Merseyside. Left afterwards with a thirty five miles ride home into a headwind, and through the none too salubrious surroundings of Leigh, Atherton and Bolton, then a mass of tram lines, trolley buses and cobblestones, a venture in the future held little attraction.

After what I'm sure all trackmen will consider the very hardest in velodrome racing, the individual pursuit, I was not for giving in without the hurly burly of the sprint handicap; an event not designed for the timid, but unfortunately I was. The track was Fallowfield, later to become the Harris Stadium. The continental bankings were new, sixty degrees, and a frightening prospect following a mid evening shower. It was only a quarter of a mile round. What was I worrying about? Though I did as I watched them carry off one contender on a stretcher in the preliminary heat. I took the allotted 'middlemarker's' position, then pulled up by toe straps tight as the holder took my weight. I remember him asking me to keep my handlebars still, and I hadn't realise they were shaking, then I looked back under my armpit to the opposition behind and watched the cool Alan Bannister, scratchman and amateur champion flexing his shoulders for the kill.

The gun went and my nerves with it! There is no quarter asked or given in a 'handicap'. Head down and go. Into the final bend and on the rails, you've caught your longmarkers and the scratchmen have caught you ..... your throat is bursting and the girls on the rails are screaming for their hero ..... it's not Bradshaw they're calling, as elbows are thrust into your ribs and the

swoop down the final bank comes and into the home straight. Someone crossed
the line first, and I know it wasn't me. I wasn't even third, the mist has never
really cleared from my eyes.
That night I was alone. The lights of Piccadilly were hazy as the city
centre passed and the bike shuddered across the uneven surface. The
middle of the city of Manchester is no place for a track machine with
number 'nought' tubular tyres, and by the time the tramlines and evil
wood 'sets' of the Rock in Bury had done their worst, I had decided.
Track racing was not for me. And it seemed the decision was unanimous;
none of my club mates were in the least interested; the road open, and
the hills in particular were our destiny.
It was our heritage. Given the escape from our valley, the climb to
Sharneyford, in Yorkshire was our goal, the climb over Dearplay Moor
when we struck for the Dales, or even the more moderate challenge, the
roads to the west or south. Whichever way, there were hills to be tackled,
and that is where we excelled.
As it appeared to racing men to the south and west of us, our club's ten
mile course, used every Thursday evening was inconceivable.
Starting high on the moor above Haslingden it plunged towards Blackburn
in a series of wild bends to the Brittania Inn and left to the turn at The King
Edward VII. The final five mile leg was vicious, with two one in ten
'pimples' to climb for good measure. Incredibly, the course record at the
time was set up by Alf Tootill at around twenty six and half minutes.
And after that burst of energy and good sport there would come a vault over
the stone wall, and, much to the consternation of the farmer's wife across the
field, a strip down, rub down, change from the sweat soaked racing gear, and
off to the Farmer's Glory for an 'O.B.J.' and the weekly 'powwow'.
Over a pint in that hostelry's tap room we set our targets. It was glaringly
obvious that in the field of hill climbing we were set to generate
supremacy; not only locally, but at an national level as time would prove. As
each autumn approached the club's name came to the fore in the cycling reports.
My own prowess in that branch of the game proved an inspiration to my team
mates. The club championship came my way for four successive years on the
Sharneyford climb, interclub honours on the 'Nick of Pendle', third then second
in the Lancashire championships and high placings in several events across the
country.
Recollections are vivid and as sharp as the autumn mist that often draped
the hills in these end of season tussles. The long journey to the Cotswolds

where an honourable third place was taken to the reigning Army Cycling Union champion, Peter Proctor, of Yorkshire, and splitting the Birmingham Olympic twins King, into second and fourth place. Of an introduction to the great Eileen Sheridan, women's champion of Great Britain now turned professional. Of a careful study of every aspect of the hill the night preceding the race, and little realising that one day, in the very near future Rossendale would have the rider to climb this very hill and be acclaimed the British champion.

CHAPTER 12

CHAMPIONSHIP SADDLES

On the grim grey slopes of the South Pennines there were accolades; the notorious Holme Moss climb where they lifted us from the saddle as we crossed the line to writhe in cramp as the ice laden fog rolled down from the moor. Brian Robinson led the Yorkshiremen on his home ground, and to myself went the honour of fastest Lancastrian, and a self esteem in the knowledge that the renowned Bob Maitland was lower in the final result. Sweet successes, as with a high placing in the national championship on Mow Cop Hill in North Staffordshire, are deep in the niches of nostalgic memorability. But perhaps deeper still are the failures. In particular, the times when one is confidently expected to win, or at least be placed in the successful first three.

Such a specific time haunts me yet. The venue was the Horse Shoe Pass in North Wales, and the event, the much publicised East Liverpool Wheelers annual hill climb. The 'cream' would be riding, and the annual turn out of the gregarious Liverpudlians would be second to none.

Of the hill, it was mine. A five mile climb in every way my dream. The hill you take your second wind after a hatefully fast start, and adjust your breathing and rhythm. The opposition was known well; there were 120 starters at the customary one minute interval and the conditions were perfect. There had been no beer the night before, only a perfect bed, and an admirable lodging in the tranquil town of Llangollen, straddling the banks of the River Dee.

The hour arrived; and then the minute. At thirty seconds you ease your arm from the shoulder of your holder, wriggle the blocks under your shoe to check the plates are gripping well to the pedal, and tighten the toe straps. Then you grip the bars..... Five..... Four..... Three..... Two..... One, and you're off. The first thirty seconds are purgatory, as the cold air fights a battle with your burning lungs, and you think of failure, of the stupidity of the game, and question your mentality. But into the first bend the shock has receded and you are back in the saddle. The first hint of the gradient ahead has you drop a gear and aggression replaces apathy. You are into your rhythm, and visions of Gino Bartalli and a breakaway on the

Col d'Izord drive you on; memories of last year when you were astride the 'tops' and overtaking the great Tom Snape for a magical few moments, and fantasies of a 'King of the mountains' jersey pulled over your head by some fabulous French film star at the close of the 'Tour de France'. Magic thoughts as you climb into the next bend, and the pass steepens sharply.

That's how it was, and the first 'gallery' was here, one mile from the start..... the first real test, and the road lined either side with a bevy of high spirited followers. It is "UP. UP. UP!" and "ALLEZ. ALLEZ. ALLEZ—" I am a shortmarker, a potential winner. They know it. They all have copies of the start sheet and we are thirty minutes apart. The sensation is ethereal, magical and highly motivating. It drove me to new heights in the art of pedal propulsion. And that's when my chain snapped, clean in half!

I'd heard of Reg Harris and Jack Spencer breaking cranks and twisting frames. THEY were twelve stone hefties, but me; a puny nine stones breaking a chain, it was unheard of.

I was still strapped tightly to the machine as it came to an undignified stop, and down I went, straight into the laps of two buxom Limehouse lovelies. They could believe it no less than I, and never ever since that time have I gazed up into a more captivating valley of Eden; at a tantalisingly less appropriate moment.

Further to these tales of adversity and consequential mirth, in retrospect, could be my brother Cyril's charge into a herd of cows at six in the morning with nothing between him and the innocent bovines, than a front wheel and saturated cycle cape. It was all so unintentional. Cyril had been demobbed from the army and a large proportion of the 'gratuity' money he invested in a spanking new bike. He had all the latest in Simplex gears and Brooks B17 'Flyer', and was immaculately shod the morning we went out at five to ride to Brock and compete in an early season '25'. The weather was far from kind however; in fact it was evil. There was a gale blowing from the west and the rain was sheeting across the moor as we strove to fight our way even downhill, to Blackburn. In due course we gave it up; there was no way we would arrive in time for timekeeper's orders.

And in consequence, the wind which had been so unkind, we now had to our backs. That would have been all very well, had it not have been pitch black. with no street lights, and battery cycle lamps that were next to useless as we hurtled down the steep drop towards Haslingden.

To have been confronted with a herd of cattle crossing the road under those conditions, with not so much as a storm lamp to warn anyone was the last thing we expected.

Whether Cyril hit anything or simply threw himself off is conjecture. I came to a stop twenty yards beyond the moving mass and counted my blessings whilst the unfortunate Cyril lifted his battered body and pile of twisted metal from the streaming roadway. I don't think he noticed me wiping the blood from his arms and legs. His concern was more the bent back forks and the S shaped front wheel we later wrenched from his erstwhile prize. Then as two burly policemen later stood on either side of the wheel in an attempt to force it back into the forks he cringed all the more. But we did ride the final miles home.

A positive reaction, although not always the most beneficial, it to take lodgings the night before an event at some nearby hostelry. A place of so called rest set by for the likes of boisterous racing folk. Such places could be Mrs. Bates at Goostrey in Cheshire; Jacks in Longridge where we slept like cowboys in a bunkhouse, or the 'ranch house' at Blythe in Nottinghamshire, where there were six beds to a room, each taking three men and each with one chamber pot only to last the night. In consequence, to the inconvenience the window was left open and a rose garden beckoned as if designed for the very purpose..... But Nicolson's at Brock, situated on the main A6 road to the North of Preston, and ultra convenient for all local events was a haven to all racing folk. It was the headquarters for all races in the locality, and in addition to changing facilities and washrooms there were rooms to be rented if you wished to stay the night. And what was of most importance, breakfasts were served in readiness for the unearthly hours that time trials were held on Sunday mornings. Which was all very well for Mr. Average. My problem was that being a railway signalman, the proximity of the main London to Glasgow west coast line, a stone's throw across the fields kept me awake virtually the night through. Trains, three times as many as we have today, were screaming by on what drivers knew as the 'race track' between Shapfell and Preston; and about the last thing for a signalman to do, was to fall asleep when trains were passing.

Three of four 'pints' in the Green Man the evening before may have helped my team mates sleep well. But where they could sweat that liquid from their bodies within five minutes of the timekeeper's word, "Go", I myself shot up in bed on the passing of every 'Duchess' or a 'Black Five' and crept down the passage to rid myself in the conventional manner. Perhaps 'Jacks' at Longridge proved the better in the end, with only competitions to who could tell the best 'smutty' joke lasting well into the night, or the perpetual rumble of half a dozen lusty snorers.

A most cherished memory of those days around the vicinity of Nicolson's returns without fail when my mind wanders to the great feats of endurance riding. I refer to the long distance road records, and in particular the ultimate; the Lands End to John O'Groats.

On this occasion Cliff Baxter and Roy Colman of the Lancashire Road Club were making the attempt to smash the tandem record, and although they narrowly failed, the sheer task, when studied closely would make the most hardened rider more than a little apprehensive. It is a non-stop ordeal, and nearly nine hundred miles of it.

A hundred of us, exhausted following a '50', lined the road at Brock when the message came they had passed through Preston. They 'steamed' by us with an extra spurt, and faded into the distance, two men alone, with but one car and an observer at the rear, and our cheers ringing in their ears.

I recall thinking them to be well into the north, until opening a map later and shuddering for them. They were not yet half way here in Lancashire, and had covered merely the 'easy bit'. Now they faced Shapfell, the Cheviots on the border, and wilds of the Cairngorms and the coast beyond Inverness. These are the feats of cycling to inspire the novice.

Often I wonder that if some member of the club had proposed allegiance to the B.L.R.C. at the time we would we have done it. The organisation was a rival body to the existing N.C.U. and not internationally affiliated and perhaps that was the cause of hesitation. But massed start enthusiasts we certainly were. I believe in general we derived more sheer enjoyment from a bunched start training run in the early season, than many of the trials against the clock which could be fought on a miserable wet morning somehwere along the dreary landscape of the East Lancashire Road and the like.

Such a 'training' run, one that would mean you wouldn't sit down before lunch time the day following, would usually call for a nine o'clock start from the Accrington bus stop; a prefabricated shelter across from the library in the centre of Rawtenstall. The itinerary went something like; the bunch of up to fifteen 'sheep' would gather and digest Jack Spencer's thesis on the overall assets of mile accumulation, then brace their muscles and prepare for the 'let's go'. Jack would suggest Jungle Cafe for lunch, a transport cafe near the summit of Shapfell, but he invariably omitted to say which way we were going; and that would inevitably be the long way.

Preston would roll by, and subsequently, Lancaster, Kendal, Windermere, and then the daunting Kirkstone Pass. The few that were still holding on to the leaders would descend in reckless abandon, and lash the pedals along

Ullswater's shores as if there was an El Dorado at the far end, then all would calm, and only the laboured breathing of the hill climber be heard on the long haul up Shapfell from the north. Perhaps five riders only would be seen lifting those huge white pint pots with the traditional blue bands. Over the one hundred and twenty miles to Jungle Cafe, the remainder could well have peeled off anywhere, and with a nonchalant shrug of the shoulders they could be met anywhere on the route home; Kendal, Ingleton, Gisburn or Burnley; but there was never time to stop; and the long climb to Rossendale; the jarring cobblestones to the Bull and Butcher and a final swoop down in Crawshawbooth, then a sprint finish at the fire station would call the end. It was all of 200 miles, but there was still time to change and gather in the Craven Heifer for a resume of the day's 'burn up' and the merits of the landlord's cherished 'Old Tom', an ale of fine old tradition in the valley. Smiles all round there would be; providing a stand was made at the bar, in preference to making any attempt to lower buttocks to benches.

Let no aspiring athlete fear the lack of bulging biceps, a six foot tanned and strapping frame, or the aura that surrounded such gifted hunks of manhood. Those were my sentiments as I clocked in a bespectacled, thin, and five foot nothing youngster on the ten mile Bury Road course. His time was a little over twenty six minutes, and close to the course record. I looked across at his bike; it still had its mudguards and bag support in place, and I glanced again at the start sheet, and at the watch I suspected had gone berserk. But no; the time was correct, and the name was Wilson; Eric Wilson, who we were destined to hear a lot more in the ensuing years.

It was 1953; Coronation Year. A year that for various reasons saw me severing connections with cycle racing. It was a regrettable decision but had to be made; and in any case my age was a little over thirty.

The last race of the previous year, a hill climb near Farnham in Surrey had been a big disappointment. Following a high placing in the national championship, a scratchmark made me a potential winner. A climb that is strewn with the wet leaves of autumn however, needs careful thought, and down went the pressure in the No. '0' track tubular tyres; and there went my hopes! Grit too, was a hazard and 200 yards out down went that front tyre onto the rim. It had been a 200 mile journey, a round trip of 400 miles; and 400 miles too far.

For this year, I would be content to organise, and at the end of the season have a final fling. It was to be the year that Rossendale first made its first combined impact in the field of National honours.

Without wasting time waiting for Wilson to request membership of the club, he was awarded the privilege there and then after his brilliant showing on the evening of his first 'ten'. This was the material we sought, and along with myself, Tootill, Higgins, Cross, Entwhistle, my brother Cyril, and the ever jovial Jack 'Sibbit' Bishop, Wilson would more than likely be the missing link that would give us national fame. How right we were. As the year progressed so did Eric and by the time we promoted our 'Coronation' open climb on the 'Nick of Pendle' he finished in a very high position, high enough to set him on his way to fame in the years to follow.

He contented himself this year by giving us but a glimpse of his potential. But he watched as we took honours in every climb in that late season. He bided his time well, and he trained hard, and with conviction and determination.

My own very last race was a non too brilliant effort on the fabled Winnats Pass in Derbyshire's Peak District. Again it was the national championship, but held two hours following the end of a twelve hour night shift thirty miles to the north; the conditions could hardly be termed favourable. I stupidly rode a 59 inch gear instead of the intended 56 but at least returned a respectable time, and led the team to a high placing, then honourably hanging up my racing shoes for the last time.

In the immediate years to follow, I read my 'Cycling' once more. In my bones I had felt the ground had been laid in what was now a distant Rossendale. The club team spirit, the dedication to give our riders the recognition they surely deserved. And there it was, staring me in the face. Eric Wilson, 'National Champion'. And what a photograph. Sitting 'on the tops', like a true 'king of the mountains', beating the country's best on a hill where once I had challenged the best. And that was not all. Wilson went on to be acclaimed National Champion no less than four times and led the Rossendale team to a convincing win on at least one occasion.

I feel I have a right to be justly proud. We set the trend, and our fruits were rich. If Johnny Palmer and those stalwarts of the original Road Club were reading that paper at the same time as I, their ankles must surely twitch in a desire to pull up the toe straps and hit the road again.

Their very own dream, now fulfilled.

CHAPTER 13

EMPTY SADDLES

Not that honour for a club's success can be placed alone on the merits of those who achieve the limelight. There are the unsung deeds of the committee members, the treasurers, the secretaries and the dedicated members who act as helpers in a multitude of ways. Any amateur organisation is only as good as its officials deem to make it. And so it was with our valley cycling clubs. If there is no-one to officiate, there is no club.

Precisely that had been the case in 1948 when the then retiring secretary of the Rossendale Wheelers, Harry Evans approached me.

He was a club rider of the old tradition. The man who approached the Sunday ride into the country in a leisurely way, and enjoyed the company of fellow members as all pottered along the byways, and along to the tea rooms of the C.T.C., and the gatherings of a multitude of assorted clubs. For a period of time he had held together what remained of the Rossendale Wheelers. The war had caused the disintegration of the Road Club, and here was what was left of the Wheelers; a matter of about twelve members, all in their teens and a majority craving guidance into the racing world.

That was not for Harry. And he was becoming older and wished to relinquish his secretaryship, but not until he found a volunteer to replace him, and one that would form a racing section and plug any thoughts of members abandoning to clubs beyond the valley with the consequential collapse of the Wheelers. It was a long tale of woe. He went on to tell me he had heard of an ability I had for organisation, though he didn't say from whom. There was an admirable treasurer in the name of John Murgatroyd, and he felt sure that should I be in any way interested, I would find it a most rewarding pastime.

He had me hooked and I became secretary; one way and another, the job lasted six years.

Significantly, I had found a vocation. In later years the experience would be turned to great advantage. Thankfully at that time I fell into it like a duck to water.

Every individual member of that wonderful dozen was a worker. Whatever task they were requested, the job was done with the minimum of fuss and by the end of a fabulous year the fortunes of the club had swung from near insolvence, to a thriving organisation boasting a membership of near a hundred and showing a bank balance high enough to secure our ventures into further fund raising activities. These were many. John Chapman proved his worth as social secretary, promoting dances at the Astoria, and when a prize draw went ahead there was found a member who had sold a grand total of 200 books of tickets, which all goes to prove the sincerity of those post war enthusiasts.

All our ventures turned to gold. Even the club magazine which pessimists forecast would be a failure. The 'Wheel' sold completely out of its one hundred a month publication, on every issue.

Intent on raising our image, the annual club dinner and prize presentation found its venue lifted from the unpretentious surroundings of a certain chip shop in Stacksteads, to the 'Con' club in Crawshawbooth, the Co-op rooms in Haslingden, and finally to the 'Royal' in Waterfoot and the 'Queens' in Rawtenstall.

And not least in the promotion of a club's image is the publicity that can be gained from the attentions of the local press. Their support is paramount and incalculable. Admitted they gain from the services of unpaid staff, though some features provided by local organisations leave a lot to be desired. Our club's press secretary did have the moderate advantage however, of a helpful friend and relation in both the Rossendale Free Press offices, and those of the 'Northern Daily Telegraph'. Drastically edited as these features can often be, they are nonetheless a club's lifeline and liaison to the public at large.

A cardinal error I have noted with some organisations I have rubbed shoulders with in recent years, is the secretary and officials distance from the membership at large. It breeds autocracy and snobbery to a high degree, and I abhor the practice. Not so was the situation in our club at the time. Far from it. We raced together, we trained together and we socialised together. Perhaps that was why, when I was moving house to a more pretentious row of private dwellings, the entire club membership turned up. It was goodbye to Primitive Terrace. Affluence we considered had hit us in a big way, and we were off to take possession of a house we were buying at the enormous figure of £750. We had put down a deposit of £75 which left nothing for the solicitor, except a promise to pay before the year was out, and in addition, no cash to employ a removal man. That was where an old hand cart, a coil of rope, and the said willing hands came in. And it went on all the evening, backwards and forwards for the one mile down Burnley Road, with chairs and wares piled high and rocking precariously from side to side. By ten at night, before the last load finally changed its home, even the local 'Bobby' lent a hand to push the last few yards on the cobbles to the rear of Woodcroft. That was after he had told us we were breaking the law, and to put a cycle lamp on the front and rear!

Alas; those uncontentious days were to end. The club had grown big. Perhaps too big. By 1951 there were opposing factions. It was a mixed club by nature of its efforts to cater for two fundamentally different forms of cycling. In fact, it was a self same situation as that arising fourteen years before, and which led to the last upheaval, and formation of the first Rossendale Road Club. And in fairness to hard working members and to a sport that was to take off in the valley with the council's support, there was a classic repeat. The Road Club was formed.

If speed was the essence, then no club could have claimed a faster take off. It was Festival of Britain year and the Mayor was anxious to part with the rate payers' money in the form of a silver trophy and give all assistance possible; and we took it willingly. Jack Holden of Bacup, Johnny Kay, Jack Harvey and Harry Ashworth of Rawtenstall all threw in financial assistance.

It was to be solely a racing club, leaving touring to the Wheelers and membership was by invitation. In that way stability and dedication to the sport was assured. As ever the cycle builder Adam Hill of Padiham was there to help the rider approaching the top. How many of us have stood in that little office over the workshop. "What angles, what rake the forks, what style lugs, and finally what colour your Hill Special?" And then gone to collect, and paid sixpence, and signed over the stamp to clear the amateur rules and status. There could be other perks to the budding amateur as well, perhaps a new tubular tyre that needs a report by the manufacturer, of an unorthodox style of racing shoe. Along with a few other riders in the area I recall us riding a trial four speed 'fixed' hub gear with splined sprocket. Quite a novelty at the time and I tried mine on the windswept Solway '50' course at Gretna in Scotland. It never made an impact as the day of the time trialists passion for fixed wheel was ending, and the continental ways taking over.

Tracing these events, I note that it was a miraculously short time before the club, as had been intended, was in a financial position to help its riders. To be entered into a national race of prestige is one thing; finding the necessary wherewithal was another. And here was where the specialist club could help.

Not only could it find the entrance fees, but club jerseys could be held for official team members, and even help with overnight accommodation charges when deemed necessary. Frankly, had help not come our way when the national championships road race was held in the Isle of Man, I doubt if ever a team would have left our shores. On that occasion admittedly, there was a strong element of luck. The race had, prior to the date been scheduled to take place on some totally unsuitable airfield in the Midlands, then at the last minute all went wrong; much to the joy of all entrants. We were all sent a free ticket for travel on the ship from Liverpool the day prior to the race; and as an afterthought on some kind official's mind, a further free invitation to the Villa Marina in Douglas, capital of the island where the one and only Joe Loss played as resident dance orchestra.

It is said that to be the unpaid secretary of any voluntary organisation is a self inflicted wound. Probably so. At the time it had not crossed my mind. It is not exactly a thankless task; although the thanks only come round once a year, at the annual dinner and prize presentation.

At the Road Club's first since its reinauguration, barely six months later, the accolades were strong in evidence to one and all; and the facts were so true. The new Road Club was a fighting force in the North West. I felt justly proud of my own achievements in the field of planning and execution. As secretary hadn't they just said so, and as they all clapped after the speech I receded a little under the table but held a secret bloat in the chest.

Likewise a similar proceeding the year following when our venue was the 'Royal' once more. The meal was excellent, the speeches by our guests Harry Aspden and Johnny Palmer superb, and the dancing and entertainment following up to perfection. All was wonderfully efficient and the secretary thanked for expertise in the entire planning.

But bad luck can befall the most meticulous of planners. The praises were still ringing in my ears the following morning as I returned to the Hotel to book the room for the following year's 'annual'. I even watched as the manager filled in the club's name and the date.

IN due course, and nine months later the wheels of organisation were put into motion. First the printing of the prestigious tickets, and the invitation to dignitaries, the booking of the band and the entertainers, the estimates for seating and the dozen associated chores. And now there was little to do but check the booking.

So I sauntered into the hotel manager's office all smiles, to be met with blank expressions when I introduced myself. No record whatsoever was there of any booking of the function room for that date by any Road Club. Indeed the room was booked for a mill owner's wedding reception..... He apologised, the hotel had changed proprietorship six months past and no list of advance bookings had been presented to the new owners..... They could do nothing! In all my time of arranging some function or other, I don't think I've ever felt such a complete nitwit. Nor have I flung myself into a bicycle saddle so quickly. At the Queen's Hotel in Rawtenstall, at that time an exclusive haunt of the well-to-do business executive and the like, I was head over heels in sheer gratitude. By untold good fortune some function of note had been cancelled for the date I required, and the management were in tears almost to a point of distraction. I reflected, could any unfortunate organiser have been so lucky?

At the printer's I met with similar luck. By the following day the tickets would have been under the press.

It was my last night as the Road Club's Secretary. None knew how near it was to my first disaster as club organiser. All was well. The night was all I wanted it to be. The success of the evening was second to none and I gazed round at the young ones, at Eric Wilson and the other lads, those who would shortly stamp their mark on the fortunes of Rossendale's cyclists. The president stood..... ''I have the honour to present this trophy to the club for annual competition''..... ''It has been inscribed the 'Bradshaw' cup, and I donate it in true thanks to the man who shall ever be remembered as Mr. Road Club.''

Days later, as I sat in the train heading for a new life in the south of England, the lump still stuck in my throat.

CHAPTER 14

BACK TO BOOTS

Nostalgia I am told, is a manifestation of happiness recalled.

Lying along on the high slopes of a Cumbrian fell. A late spring sun burning deep into the naked flesh, and a gentle breeze stirring the brown tufts of the upland grass. A deep hollow, and the magical resonance of a tumbling beck. A haven of utter tranquillity for the would be dreamer.

Far from the plains of Southern England, now my home, I pondered. Fifteen years had lapsed since that hour of farewell. A parting with a life in the great outdoors. Now here I was. The legacy had brought me back. A return to the roots, where a man can search his soul.

Should I be seeking passion or pathos, or simply to recline in sheer musical paradise, then it is to Giuseppi Verdi I heed; if it is pure inspiration I need, then to Beethoven I turn. And that is what had transpired, some evening or two previously. I believe it was his symphony, the Eroica, that turned my thoughts from the materialistic, to normality.

And here I was, casting thoughts to the days of the cycle and the rucksack. Wanting to shed the care of domestication and the hectic business environment that had pulled me into its mesh.

My railway work had sent me south, with the motivation, as with every parent to earn more, and more money for a growing family and, all the needs of a fast changing society.

Admittedly for the first five years the bike was constantly at my side; but as a necessity, rather than a form of sport or pleasure. It was ridden with regularity the sixteen miles to work, but apart from that I shunned the idea of its other uses. Indeed in a successful attempt to blot out the erstwhile memories of a once idolised lifestyle, the deed had gone as far as burning certificates. In hindsight, an act of crass stupidity. They were momentoes of rides which at the time were deeply symbolic, as instance the establishment of the Waterfoot to Blackpool and back record; the Waterfoot to Settle, and the climbs on Nick O' Pendle and Sharneyford.

At that time it was a self inflicted disfranchisement, a call from the inner senses of moral duty, and to those ends I went. There could be no vision of Ron Bradshaw, open air fanatic and crazed pedal pusher pounding the roads of pastoral Wiltshire, it was far cry from the magnetic charm of the Dales country or the wild downhill swoops from the high Pennines, anyway.

Now, long hours at work, a wonderfully patient wife and two lovely children were creating the desired effect. Added to that, a keen interest in music, and a desire to make something of an old terraced house we took in Swindon town tempered, then finally halted the urge to wander.

When the ultimate came, and the old racing bike was sold to raise capital in a business venture, even that failed to pull a tear. The disease had in the end dispersed and melted into a timeless infinity.

Time rolled by, another son was born, and more and more the call of a curlew, or the resonant sound of a tumbling stream diminished. It seemed the new lifestyle, the motor car, the dining out, the trappings of the affluent sixties and what else seemed the 'in thing', and the road to the 'rat race' loomed. The holiday on the 'costa' or the cruise on the 'Med'. Those were the priorities of the day.

Too large are the temptations, and too long are the hours you work to achieve this end. The sting in the tail will nip the unwary, ere he reaches his elusive El Dorado.

In that hollow on the approach to Great Gable I was recovering from that near fatal sting, and it had been both instinct, and the legacy that drew me once more to my heritage. To Blea Tarn I had returned to a paradise; nothing I know in this life will ever dim the sight and sounds of that shimmering gem of water lying tranquil in the moonlight, guarded only by the slopes of shadowy fells, and the towering bulk of the 'Langdale Pikes' stark against a cobalt sky. It could have changed. But it hadn't. Perhaps it never will. Only the infernal motor car will challenge the serenity of milieus so sacred. And even this predator will disappear as night unfolds, or perhaps does not even come at all, as the heavens open, the rain lashes across the mountains, or the snow lies deep in the ghylls, when only the muffled bleat of a forlorn lamb is heard. The ewe gasps her last as a cruel Lakeland winter takes its toll.

It is then, as in all climes, the majesty of these Cumbrian Fells pull a romantic, and a wanderlust within their spell.

I had walked alone, as I so often do. There is neither need to slow the pace for a novice, or speed up for the impatient. My camera and my thoughts, the docile sheep, and the call of a bird, these were my companions. From the lonely shore of Styhead Tarn I gazed across its placid waters, to scan the shimmering silhouette of Great End and its brooding crags. Then from the tarn, to that little hollow where the rest would come sublime.

The boots and the socks were first to come off. Boots I hadn't worn for fifteen years, and I was now paying the price. Then with a total spontaneity the rest came off. Every mortal stitch; and sun gave that stimulus; the catalyst that unfailingly has been my benefactor since that very day. I am not an atheist, I am not an unbeliever, maybe I am an agnostic. Whatever it be, had I been pagan, then Mithras would have been my sun god.

I was infinitely happy. There is no shame in nakedness. It rests only in the mind of the sordid, or the misguided conventionalist. Today, I was happy to allow those health giving rays to reach every inch of a naked body that in the first displayed itself with total abandon, and received less than one word of ghastly disapproval.

In this state of total abandon, and pure euphoria, there is time abundant to allow nostalgia to run its full course. To take one to more carefree days than those when pounds and pennies seem the sole reason for our existence upon this earth. I lay back and mused. Into what some may say is a silly lapse into bygone pleasures. But to me it was a return to reality; a reason to swear never, to desert this life of dedication to the wide open spaces ever again. Should the cycle have ceased to be my mode of employ, then a return to the leanings of Ward Ogden, and the happy days of walking the hills with a backpack, these could easily be accomplished.

In the days of less affluence, there were by far the closer friendships. The motor car it is that divides us today. The impersonal status symbol we use to show our superiority, and few fellow travellers had spoken to me in the valley below, where a shining estate car marked the territory I had claimed; but here, on the wild slopes, all were one. Like the bonds that existed on our terraced row in Crawshawbooth. Where all laughed together at each others fortunes or mishaps. Somehow the mishaps brought the greatest mirth.... The morning when Joe, our next door but one neighbour ran downstairs clad in his nightshirt only, to take the newspaper from the letter box. It was stuck, so he opened the door in order to pull it from the outside, and with such gusto he did, the door slammed to with the catch down, and left poor Joe marooned on the pavement. He had two problems, one, it was an extremely windy morning, and the other that his wife had gone off to work and he had no means of getting back indoors. Only the kindness of Mrs. Finney on the other side saved the situation..... She took him in and sheltered him with discretion whilst another neighbour ran to the mill for the key..... Then it was not his day in the end. The coalman later in the morning lifted the wrong grate and ten hundredweights of best 'Yorkshire' landed in OUR coal cellar instead of his.

There were the embarrassing times. There was a war on, and shortages were rife. When someone dropped our chamber pot it was a tragedy; it was a case of a 'penny bus ride' to the row of toilets at the end of the street, or if you were desperate there was the enamel bucket closeted discreetly at the head of the cellar steps. But this chamber pot was the china one! The one with the ornate pattern and a charming tinkle. And I wasn't expecting half the 'street' to be out chattering the day I brought a miserable 'utility' plain brown replacement back home tied to the back of my saddle bag. Twenty miles I'd ridden to get one, and in wartime they didn't even have the paper to wrap it up in.

Embarrassment in itself was little known anyway in our commune of some twenty houses. There was the newly married couple at the end, eager on return to tell us all of their amusing anecdotes after an eventful honeymoon. The funniest was the saga of the 'Cherry Blossom' boot polish. It must be pointed out that this was long before our chemist shops were packed with every conceivable aid to the science of sexual intercourse. A so called 'French letter' or 'Durex' was all that was available, and for even that, one looked over the shoulder to see no-one was about, and that the shop was empty before creeping in and requesting one from under the counter. Thus when one required some form of lubricant for either the rubber sheath or for the recipient's comfort, there was no such substance available. Then the inevitable tin of 'Vaseline' was the collective answer. And that is what our friends took along in their suitcase. The trouble then arose, with suitable Victorian modesty the couple undressed in the dark, and she, later in suitable abandoned desire, leaned out of the bed and took out the little round tin from the case.

How the two tins contrived to lay side by side is immaterial. The resulting ravages to a set of crisp white cotton sheets though can well be imagined, as well the consternation of our two friends. Passion plunged to an all time low as early morning light revealed the worst, and the sight of two black and white naked bodies running pell mell down the corridor to the bathroom not an acceptable Sunday morning occurrence, even in the enlightened town of Blackpool.

The subject of condoms brings to mind a small chemist's shop in Yorkshire Street, Rochdale near to where I was working at the time. Here a gentleman clad in a white coat was always in attendance behind the counter, I had known no-one else. And to him I would go and request a 'washable' rubber sheath, as the little packet of 'three' was becoming rather expensive. As was the custom, a little peep inside, and there was no-one about; so I went in. Lo and behold, from behind the counter up popped a smiling face; that of a sweet sixteen year old girl who spelled the very image of innocence. "Yes," she requested. I was trapped. "Have you a washable durex?" I stammered. "Yes," she beamed, "small, medium or large?" I was transfixed. Not knowing whether to brag, or be ashamed, I took the easy way out and stated 'medium'. I have often wondered whether that girl was a innocent as she appeared.

To reminisce, alone and in such wonderful surroundings is ecstatic; incredibly I realised that when tramping and cycling these hills and valleys in yesteryear the very thought of ever possessing a car was nonsensical. The bike and the boots would be my sole means of travel forever; but that was yesterday.

Good as nostalgia is for the soul, too much sun on naked flesh can neutralise the gain. The boots, the clothes and the rucksack were on again, and it was to Esk Hause, Sprinkling Tarn and Rossett Gill the path took me. Into the lonely head of Mickleden where the scree of Pike O' Stickle tumbles to the floor of Stake Pass, and the track leads me on to Dungeon Ghyl, and more memories here in the old hotel.

It was here, and with Dorothea, after a hair raising descent from Pavey Arc in a force nine gale we had arrived exhausted many years previously. We were almost catapulted the entire length down Mill Gill, and straight into the bar of this hostelry where two pints of cider dropped unceremoniously into two extremely empty stomachs; we then rolled leglessly on to Stool End Farm and a much belated dinner.

That was when the 'unclassified' road over to Little Langdale, and the passes of Wrynose and Hard Knott were still surfaced in shale. No tarmacadam to steady the wheels when you plummeted into Duddon Bottom. The tracks and the loose grit had you tumbling and sliding the length from top to bottom.

With the 'mountain' bike, and even the car traversing these tracks far from anyone's mind, we held the vision of this sanctuary untouched into the far foreseeable future. But now it had arrived, an internal combustion engine that would ere long churn up the tracks, smash the heavenly silence and pollute the hillsides with deadly fumes. Come too, would the flocks of sightseers in their glass enclosed cages, to throw out lighted cigarettes and plastic bags, and desecrate the countryside they neither knew, nor cared for little.

On the whole I wondered, though my own musings would be irrelevant. If the more remote areas of this gem of national park land were made inaccessible to the motor vehicle, with the sole exception of the emergency services; could we not return to the principles of the old Y.H.A. when access to your overnight accommodation was by foot or cycle only, in other words, under your own steam? The hills and tracks would be free to the genuine country lover, and to the farmer, the shepherd, the birds and the wildlife, then without that motor car, little would be lost, and an age regained.

I had rested. I had recovered a legacy of a massive heart attack. The answer had been blowing in the wind. And now the dormant embers were rekindled. We would tramp the hills once more, and if the depths of pastoral Wiltshire did little to inspire the fell walker, then with a shrug of apology to the engine I oft decry, we would sally froth to the base of some wild mountain or moor. Not too distant were the green hills of mid Wales.

And in the fullness of time, I would live to realise the significance of those early reflections of our 'land of song'.

CHAPTER 15

CUMBRIAN BOOTS

To the once hardened fell walker there is little of note wandering the confined paths of the Berkshire and Wiltshire Downs. Apart from a magnificent view of the Vale of the White Horse from the vicinity of that pre-Roman deity, and the pure joy of exercise, it is predatory. On the other hand, it loosened our limbs, and served as a stimulus.

In the course of my business, a job that entailed driving endless miles across the length and breadth of England and Wales, I had often been intrigued by the long line of hills that stand out so prominently against the sky line when travelling the plain of Worcester. They lay twix the Cotswolds and the Black Mountains of South Wales. Travelling even by train on the Midland Line that abutts the A38 and M5, and with a rising sun and clear sky to the west, they entice the man with itchy feet. In particular, when he is sat in his little glass bubble, and can do very little about it. They were the Malvern Hills. At the first opportunity I did something about it.

It was following a lecture from Dr. Watkins, and a period of extra long working hours. Grant yourself two or three days break at least every two months admonished he, and who was I to argue. There had been sufficient hospital wards and neurology centres passed my way in the last eighteen months. So I would do it, and do it in style. Out came the Jaguar, and into the boot went the rucksack, suitable footwear and spare clothing.

The fact that I made straight for the most pretentious hotel in the town of Ledbury subtly reflects the image that affluence at that time had created. The 'Feathers' is an imposing Tudor building on the town's High Street, and I slid the 'Jag' into the allotted space behind. A stately bedroom was shown to me, and captivated by the view into the town's busy High Street and the old market place I settled for it. The period decor, the luxurious bed and the panelled walls were exquisite. It was a taste of a bygone age. Elizabethan I felt sure. One almost awaited arrival of the serving maid and the jug of mead or mulled wine.

An hour in the residents' lounge, in the company of the 'Times', the 'Telegraph' and a buxom widow of aristocratic descent preceded a sumptuous meal, and finally a carafe of the best 'vin de maison'. Good conversation with the lady of aristocratic leanings, and a generous 'tipple' of the best Napoleon Brandy followed, and the evening ended with 'good nights' all round at about midnight.

What an excellent way to prime a three day walking tour I considered. None of those cold baked beans and a stale crust of bread at Black Sail hut under the shadow of Pillar Rock, or a plate of tepid half cooked porridge in the damp confines of Fulshaw Hostel on the bleak moors of the East Pennines. No; this was really living!

I steadied myself up the creaking, winding staircase; into my room, and between the snug perfumed sheets, to slumber along until dawn;..........
Or so I had visualised. By two in the morning all was reality. Gone were the visions of Elizabethan tranquillity and the clip clopping of an isolated cavalier's horse down the High Street. Now there was a cavernous twentieth century articulated monster droning down the road. It was the Bulmer's Cider lorry, and they would pass every half hour. I got to timing them with my watch! A mild screech of the air brakes, then a double de-clutch down through all the gears and a rumble round the corner onto the Tewkesbury road. Up through two gears now, and an ear-piercing plod up the hill in front. Hardly had the distant drone died away, when it seemed the next one approached. Through heavy eyelids I gazed at a plate of kippers for breakfast. Different I mused; perhaps the shock would help clear a befuddled mind. Though at least I had the presence of mind to have my room changed, and if the surrounds were not to be of the same elegance, it was to be certain I would sleep.

The charm of these pleasant hills captivated me. From the highest point, on the 'Worcestershire Beacon' one looks down directly to the resplendent spa town of Great Malvern, to the west are the Black Mountains of Breconshire across the border, and to the east the lower line of the Cotswolds. Here, at a height of a mere 1,395 feet and gazing to where the sun rises, no other contour matches that on which you stand; not until the Ural Mountains in distant Russia break the flat expanse. From a little to the north of this point, and south for several miles are unrestricted walks and by bringing the car each day to a different area the entire chain of hills were covered in either direction over a period of three days. They were extremely pleasant days too; the weather was most kind and the walking a welcome therapy. That was until the final day, almost the final hour, when despite tramping the millstone grit, and the granite uplands of the north, the endless tufts of coarse moorland and paved Roman roads without ever a mishap, here, on the gentle green slopes of a midland hillside, down I went.

Resisting the temptation to remove the boot, the laces were tightened suitably and I hobbled to the car. At least the entire walk had been accomplished and

that pleased me most. The ankle was not broken, only a severe strain and when
the heavy swelling disappeared some days later, all was back to normal.

So much so, that within a few weeks, I was sitting on the edge of Whitehorse
Hill near Uffington, when the idea of a walking trip in the Fens first crossed
my mind. Why ever my thoughts should have turned in that direction I shall
never comprehend. Possibly it came about because I was staring across the
Vale, watching the tell tale smoke of a distant train as it raced along Brunel's
great route to the west. For the twenty miles from Didcot Junction to Swindon
you follow its progress over the plain. Then gazing to the north east, there was
nothing but more plains, an infinity of pastoral field, hedge and produce.
That's all there was no doubt. But should a man be biased? Was my criticism
warranted? Shouldn't a man set foot in a land before he condemns? Then that
I would.

And so it came about. And in retrospect I will say, should any man of the hills;
of the tumbling streams and the mountain and lake, ever lack appreciation of
the land he inherited, then send him to those characterless marshes of the
Norfolk Broads. For the boatman or the motorist, for the pub enthusiast or the
cyclist who abhors hills then it is the place. But it is not for the hillman. The
more I saw of these flatlands, the more tantalising emerged the visions of
Lakeland, and the hills of the Celtic 'fringe'.

The 1970's were here and soon would come the county re-planning, and a
return to the ancient Cambro-British principalities. In Wales the shires would
disappear, and in Lakeland their kinsmen would see the name of Cumbria
return. Furness, the northern spur of Lancashire, the eastern corner of
Northumberland and the entire county of Westmorland now would take the
name of the Cymraeg, a folk there long before the invading Saxon and
Norseman..... I wondered if they would have a ceremony at the 'Three Shires
Stone', at the summit of Wrynose Pass. Doubtful I mused; in all probability
the bureaucrats sat in their pinned striped suit behind desks in three shire halls
had never heard of it.

About this period in time Dorothea had opted for a course of typewriting
at the local evening classes in Wootton Bassett. This was in effect to help
me out in my business, as I am both the world's worst typist, as well as
being its worst speller of the English language. But like me, she was
becoming 'longer in the tooth' and such displays of concentrated strain were
now repugnant. In case of which she was talked into transferring to the art
class, and found a new vocation overnight. She became inescapably lured, and
in a short space of time landscapes, with an emphasis on lake and mountain

became her chosen subject.

Within acceptable limits, that was my own good luck. I avidly snatched up the camera, and suggested that my next trip out should be to Cumbria where a host of suitable material could be recorded, and later set to canvas. It was agreed and I awaited patiently the views of the weatherman.

Before long he obliged, a ridge of high pressure was moving in from the west and we could expect settled weather for the next few days.

With that I was off. And by lunch time the day following lay basking in the sun high on the slopes of Bow Fell. At close to 3,000 feet this is a phenomenon not often experienced in a country unfortunately denied its fair share of sunshine.

In no way the ascetic I once was, and with the onset of late middle age, the desire to sleep on boulder strewn hillsides, in rowdy youth hostel dormitories, or even in the back of the car had diminished in the mists of time. On this occasion the comforts of the new Dungeon Gill Hotel were more to my taste. A hostelry that even in my wildest flights of fancy, I never dreamed would see the likes of me crossing its threshold. Then again, an infinity of water had plunged from Skelwith Force since the first time I cycled this road with half a crown in my pocket.

I needed nourishment, not punishment, and on this morning I had left in a wonderfully exuberant frame of mind.

Mill Gill, tumbling carelessly down from Stickle Tarn, and the glorious backdrop of Pavey Arc glistened in the early sun. Past Stool End Farm I strode, and shortened the pace on the slow climb on the Band. Through the gap, and to the first glimpse of Eskdale, then the final push and you are on the summit of Bow Fell, at 39 feet below the 3,000 contour.

Facing you now, is, in my opinion, the most spectacular of all the lakeland high peak panoramas. It is what I call 'the arc', and no doubt others do likewise. Across the barren upper Esk Valley, flanked by a sheer mass of granite rise the awesome crags of Scafell Pike, England's highest peak at 3,210 feet; but now, despite a brilliant blue sky in every one direction, the summit garlanded itself in a ring of cloud.

For the photograph I wanted, and indeed had tried for over many a year, I would wait, and wait.....

I stretched out, leaned on an elbow and gazed into the valley beneath. Wile and remote. A haven for the climber and the outdoor pursuitist. Where Eric Shipton, or was it Frank Smythe, of Everest fame had inaugurated the first outward bound school. Over to my left the lonely 'three tarns' and the distinctive Crinkle Crags, whilst beyond loomed the cap of 'The Old Man of Coniston', Lancashire's highest point at 2,633 feet. Hidden behind this rugged foreground are the sylvan waters of Coniston Lake, a burial water for the late Donald Campbell who died in 1967 attempting to smash the world's water speed record.

Yet this fantasmagoria is dwarfed, as one turns to scan the west and the north. The majesty, the magnetic awesomeness that meets the eye is unchallenged. Sombre and fearsome even in idyllic conditions, in the twilight of winters day it is evil, frightening; yet somehow irresistible. The vicious angles of rock buttressed on 'Lords Rake' and 'Broad Stand' brought a reminiscent shudder. Years previously, with only the faintest trace of a track from the summit, I had picked my way off the mountain in a snowstorm. Along with Dorothea we had kicked the snow from stone after stone, to find the tell tale scrape of a clinkered boot; then gone from blessed cairn to cairn until finding safety on lower ground.

Those were the times one well recalls; but today all was bliss; I still awaited the kind removal of that stupid cloud, tantalising as it was, shrouding every inch of my chosen subject. Perhaps if I hid the camera back in the rucksack that would help.

I glared at the thing, and in time became fascinated. Seemingly there was something to be learned about the formation of a cloud. Along with the layman, clouds I had imagined to be a string of ugly black things that formed over the Atlantic and were blown from there by the prevailing wind and dumped unceremoniously over our country ad lib, eventually to be replaced by a clear sky when the wind had done its job. Apparently not quite so. Here, as I have observed on many an occasion since when watching other of the highest peaks of an area, the sky was perfectly clear as far as the eye could see, yet the one and only cloud rested virtually immovable on this, the highest point. With patience the process can be witnessed. The vapour slowly drawn from the streams and damp forests below, resting on the high peak as a newly formed cloud, then disappearing mysteriously into thin air. That no doubt, where the adage arose.

By three in the afternoon, I despaired; there would be no photograph today. How prudent I pondered, is it that the man with the camera walk alone. The frustrations he holds would be nothing, to those of a companion kicking his heels in desperation, to say nothing of the score of misadventures that dog the life of the enthusiast.

In the course of seeking the best angle, the position of the sun, or the masking of jet lines in the sky I have fallen into streams, slithered on my backside down icy slopes, walked into a teaming pile of freshly deposited cow dung, and dangled from the verandah of a fast moving Spanish train in the high Sierra. All in the name of amateur photography. Yet it is all good fun and for almost all the years of keen interest a tripod was never in my possession. Unlike the youth of today, who walks about with video camera, bags of various zoom lens and the like, the cost of a tripod was exorbitant to us, and in any case the sheer bulk of these lattice wooden structures would have made its carrying a nightmare..... No, the art was in balance; the precarious piling of a half dozen stones, leaning two bikes together and using the saddle, or having the assistance of a low wall. And with the added benefit of the new self timing devices the likes of we loners were ably provided, though the amusing results could sometimes give momentary annoyance. The exposures could result in a view of Sty Head Tarn tilting at an alarming angle, and about to spill its entire waters across the horizontal crags of Great End and Lingmell. Or there could be a shot of myself, totally out or focus and still attempting to prop up the front of the camera with a couple of spent match sticks.

Now, at last, and to complete the saga of a half day's suspense, the cloud on our subject Scafell Pike dispersed; but with that, round came the sun; and directly in line with the lens! I gave it up. Tomorrow I would try Gable, and by lunch time I had done that, perched high above Napes Needle with the ever enticing panorama from that vantage point spread boundless in every direction.

Wastwater, England's deepest lake lies two thousand feet below you, and behind are an unending sea of peaks into the horizon. The waters of Wasdale, like those of Hawswater are the least visited by the motorist, and a haven for the walker and climber. For the uninitiated it can be daunting. There are the challenging walks by the hundred, turn half right and drink in the vista, Kirk Fell, Pillar, Steeple, Red Pike; Black Sail Pass, and across the head of Ennerdale, to Scarth Gap and over to the 'Hay Stacks'. Had Dorothea been with me today she would have taunted me yet again for the time I led her, half exhausted as a first time hiker along the unending track down Ennerdale and to the elusive hostel on the banks of that lonely lake.

As the day progressed ample camera shots presented themselves, and from Sprinkling Tarn I made Rossett Gill, and eventually Stake Pass and to High White Stones and the banks of Easdale Tarn. Here, there are excellent views, contrasting to say the least, from those of lonely Wasdale head. The impressive bulk of the Helvellyn range, with the central focus on Helvellyn itself, at 3,118 feet it lay open to the dreams of the wanderer. That could be another day. For now, I was content to strip off, soak up the sun, and lie in contemplation. It was fitting farewell to a country I adored, yet in all probability would not set foot in for another decade.

CHAPTER 16

WELSH BOOTS

The deceptively high, albeit predominantly grass covered hills of Breconshire are a far cry from the rugged crags of their sisters in the Cambrian regions to the north.

It so happened that due to circumstances of business we had moved from the plains of Wiltshire to the green hills and the fertile valleys of Mid Wales. It was the type of move I had secretly yearned for since ever having had to leave the slopes of the West Pennines.

Here we both sensed a return to our heritage. The pure air of the mountain, the timeless babble of the upland river, and the call of the night owl. Here there were people too, who tilled the land and reared the sheep; ever keen to help a stranger, and with no single thought of a financial return. Far from the commercial centres, and the nests of the rat race; here where the car had its use in the community, and never found display as the shining status symbol.

Accepted without question, we had settled quickly, and soon we were scanning the surroundings; the challenge was limitless. Granted there would be little chance to put any planned walks into practice in the immediate future; we had a business to establish, but map study, and the odd reconnoitre by car would suffice for the meantime.

Throughout the first two years we had stood in our spare moments, and stared; the views were irresistibly captivating. Surrounded as we were by the Carmarthenshire Black Mountains to the east, and directly in front lay the entire ridge of the Brecon Beacons, the choice was phenomenal. If that was not enough of a good thing, to the north flowed the Wye from its source on Plynlimmon, and a little to the west rose the Usk on the slopes of Bannau Brycheiniog. Altogether a tremendously impressive territory for the intrepid walker.

It may have been two years later, but in due course the time came, and the dust was shaken from the rucksack and boots; we were able to strike out straight from the front door, something that would have raised an inquisitive eyebrow in the middle of Swindon town. A 'loosener' was needed, and a ten mile plod along the shores of Llangorse Lake and along the Myndd Troed, suitable as a starter.

In contrast to nearby walks of that nature, there were to be tough hikes in the 'fans' beyond, but they would come in good time. We knew well not to underestimate those mountains. They were not the rugged peaks of North Wales, Cumbria or the highlands of Scotland, but nevertheless needed a vast amount of caution. Their grassy slopes at up to 3,000 feet hid many a trap for the unwary of unprepared. Only recently a member of the prestigious S.A.S. had lost his life on the heights we scanned from the comfort of our own lounge, this highlighted but one of many tragedies. Recalling an incline of the ear to the crackling radio as a child, so often would I hear a report of someone missing on the wastes of Kinder Scout in Derbyshire, or the mysterious lands of the Black Mountains in South Wales.

For the present time however, we opted for walks on the lower slopes, and intriguing as it was, the Allt-yr-Esgair ever beckoned from our lounge window. The 'Allt' as it was locally known rose into conical flanks from the edge of the lake, and was ever a magnet to our guests. In any business there are gimmicks to be sought and ours, as caterers was a dessert, awarded the distinctive title "Peach yr Esgair" in tribute to the hill the diners viewed as they slipped their spoons into the chocolate topped pyramid of peach and cream. With total disregard, only one, of the hundred and one quests served our little speciality, ever thought to ask the meaning of the neologism.

Be that as it may, to us the 'Allt' was ever our focal point. Neither did we ever tire of gazing at it, or from it. Casting your eye from the summit in any direction whatsoever the panorama is exquisite. Awesome no, breathtaking, the more appropriate superlative. A superb vista of the winding River Usk from Crickhowell to Abergavenny in the east, and to the town of Brecon and the borders of Carmarthenshire westwards. The beckoning fingers of the 'Beacons', to the fore, whilst behind, the escarpment of the brooding Black Mountains, all give shelter from a biting east wind, to Cwm Fforest and the village of Cwm Du, the 'Black Valley'. From the Mynydd Troed across to the heights of Waun Fach, the eye scans, to the loftiest point, and to the renowned 'Sugar Loaf' (Y Fai).

Here then was the perfect and natural verandah to sit, and to plan our onslaughts into the very heart of Mid Wales. We did it with care and forethought, and in the remaining ten years whilst residing in that wonderful corner of the land, the peaks of almost every hill and mountain in the old shires of Brecknock, Carmarthen and Monmouth had been trodden.

Pen-y-Fan, our highest mountain at a little under 3,000 feet did not deserve the insult of the many ill shod picnickers, who bravely deserted their cars at the Storey Arms, half way up the mountainside, plodded their weary way up the rather monotonous southern approach, and then returned after depositing their plastic rubbish on the summit. No; it rightly deserves the frontal climb from Cwm Gwdi or from Cwmcynwyn to do justice.

Another approach of note is from Bryn Teg and Cribbin, and on the first occasion we took that route, we were accompanied by Fred and Nora, the lifelong lovers of open spaces we have met in earlier chapters. .... Nora is a connoisseur in the art of tea making; and, in the choice of the leaf, the country of origin, and where, when or where not to 'brew up'. She carried her knowledge to great lengths; even to the summit of Pen-y-Fan. And whilst there is a small silver teapot ever residing in the bottom of her rucksack, she denies not the use of a plastic mug. But there again, tea bags are taboo, and only the best leaf shall be deposited in the silver treasure which has been previously swilled round with a precious quarter mug of near boiling water from the vacuum flask. Should there be a few 'floaters' on the surface after the sacrificial 'brew', then there is no worry, she is an adamant follower of my down to earth farmer friend Vic, who states what goes in at one end will surely come out at the other; it matters little so long as the ultimate taste is 'just right', and 'par excellence'.

Not realising all this, the crowd that was assembled by the cairn on that windy lunchtime gasped in amazement as she calmly threw off her rucksack and set out the polished silver pot, the embroidered tray cloth and plastic mugs! In particular, as not one member of the assembly was British anyway. But that is Nora; wind, rain, hail or snow, and wherever she be, her inbuilt timing mechanism will call a halt at four in the afternoon, and out will come the teapot.

Having reached this highest point in South Wales, and given the better of conditions, then the panorama is indeed extensive. Away in the distant north is the Cader Idris (Arthur's Seat) in Snowdonia, whilst in the central foreground, the green slopes of Plynlimmon and Hafren Forest rise, and cradle the source of Britain's longest river, the Severn. Swinging completely round the coastline of both Wales and England are clearly etched, and there spills the Severn into the Channel, having traversed a grand winding course of some two hundred miles from a fount you can visualise by the mere flick of a head.

It may not be every senior citizen's idea of a sixty fifth anniversary walk, but I am a determined person. The hike was a fifteen mile or more of high ridge walking, and one I had sworn to do ever since setting foot in this National Park. It is one I would recommend to anyone with reasonable experience, but a car, the object on which I cast so many aspersions, and a driver are necessary. That is unless you are young, fit and capable of the round trip.

As for myself, I was reasonably fit, but by no means young, and roped in the services of Dorothea and the car!

Of course, it was the view from the house that had ever been the inspiration. I could pick out half the route with the binoculars, and by the end of the day that I finally achieved it, I could well have been the sorest man in our village; though I'm sure I was one of the happiest.

From the site of the old Torpantau railway station where I was dropped off, the track climbs from the 1,000 foot contour to 2,500 at Craig-y-Fan Ddu and Waen Ridd, then holds these contours in general to the successive peaks of Craig Cwm Oergwm, Fan Big, Cribbin, and on to Pen-y-Fan and the last peak Corn Du. By that time the limbs are beginning to creak a little and I confess the return to Fan Big and the long descent into the village of Llanfrynach did little to encourage thought of any further exercise on that day; with perhaps the exception of lifting a pint glass in the Tap Room of the Black Cock.

Seemingly the car was becoming a strong factor in the aid to forays into the mountains; as in this case, Dorothea had met me at Llanfrynach, and the day ended a complete success. It had its uses too in planning future walks, as in the event of our first reconnaissance of the Breconshire Black Mountains. Although that first sortie did turn out to be somewhat a black comedy.

At the time we had not lived long in the area and I still pursued my job as a wholesale textile merchant. Trade was difficult and I had found myself working seven days a week in order to keep things ticking over. Thus my tale of woe was being unfolded in the confines of the Black Cock one evening, when one and all of the bar proppers came up with a unanimous suggestion. "Have a day off, Ron; get away from it all; take Dorothea over the Gospel Pass in the Black Mountains. She'll love it."

And so it came about. A rare thing for me to do about the time, we loaded the car for a picnic, and as it was mid week and also late September, there would be few about. All was set for a day's carefree meander along the leafy lanes and sylvan glades that abound in that little corner of old Monmouthshire.

The road heads north from Abergavenny and onto the route of Gospel Pass, a twenty mile stretch of single track road that hosts a hundred retreats. A euphoria for one who seeks tranquillity and respite. At Cwmyoy the little church with its leaning tower and nave to visit. In Llantony the ruins of the priory, and all the time a gentle autumn breeze rippling the grassy slopes of these border hills. It was serene. Far from the pressures of a company desk, the telephone, the account books and the V.A.T. returns. The sun shone and we planned our walks for the future. On our right was the Offas Dyke long distance footpath straddling the ridge of Hay Bluff, and ahead the last few yards of the Pass before plummeting into Hay-on-Wye. Then on to the horizon came a car, its windscreen glinting in the afternoon sun.

It was the first one we had seen in the last two hours; there were passing places however. He went into one! and I went into one, He flashed, and I flashed! It seemed stalemate, so I drove out; so did he! It was all so courteous, and then we rounded the hidden bend, both of us, that is, and all but met in head on collision.

I stared down my bonnet and we were barely a car length apart as he wound down his window. He had a big smile..... "Mr. Bradshaw," he called..... Oh, no! I shuddered..... The eternal travelling salesman, Mr. Brown from Bristol. "Been looking all over for you," he beamed. "Went into that little pub in your village; the lady told me where I'd find you!"..... Is there ever a hiding place, I mused.

At that we backed up to the clear passing place, and there at two thousand feet above sea level, on the open slopes of the Mynydd Twmpa the deal was done. Within ten minutes he was on his way again, smiling as ever, and with an order for one hundred dozen men's wool socks.

More often than not our aspect of these particular mountains was from the west or the north. From our bedroom window which faced east the first thing every morning was to view the escarpment; it told us much of the weather we could expect that day, and not only that, the view forever served as a golden magnet.

One of the winters we experienced at that time was a particularly hard one. Snow remained in cwms for long into the spring, and even early summer; in fact it was June 6th that year when the last trace disappeared; an easy date for those of our age group to recall. We bided our time. I knew that one day we would tread the heights of Waen Fach tantalisingly hidden from view by the bulk of Mynydd Troed, and patience was rewarded on retirement some five years later.

It signalled a new phase in our attitudes to the use of the motor car. In fact on many occasions the vehicle would be our bed for the night. Though in these local Black Mountains home was never far away.

Notably here, as with many areas of the central Cambrians, the few narrow roads peter out, falling far short of the high ground. This is a windfall to the likes of us; a heaven sent spot to leave the car, change into hiking gear, return windswept and hungry to a welcome flask of tea, or even put down our heads for the night.

Habitually we put the scheme into practice. First one cwm and then the next until every peak from the Sugar Loaf to Mynydd Bychan, and from Waen Fach to Pen Allt-Mawr had been traversed. From the heights of Y Das we thrilled as the coin was reversed; now, after a long and patient wait we looked DOWN at our house; Far in the distance, a dot among a sea of oaks and but a speck so close to the shores of the lake.

There is a such a profound lack of walkers among these hills. We often had them entirely to ourselves. So unlike the slopes of the Pennines and the fells of Cumbria. Their geographical position, no doubt, far from the centres of dense population is the over-riding answer. It was probably our good fortune. Left alone to seek, and to discover, there are many surprises. Like the multitude of tiny churches that rarely find mention in the guide books.

One in particular caught our imagination. It is the lonely structure at the foot of Y Das at Llanelieu, where Mrs. Patterson of the mountain pottery holds the key. Behind it is a building by the name of Ty Du, in English, the Black House!..... The very soul of these hill people lie in these hidden buildings, and the high abandoned farmsteads, and the epitome to a fast fading way of life hereabouts, I found portrayed to perfection, in a sad, but extremely powerful play on television in recent years. It's title simply 'Morgan'!

Whilst a most spectacular view of this particular range can be taken from high on the road between Beaufort and Llangynidr, given the clarity and suitable position of the sun; the Black Mountain of Carmarthenshire, the Mynydd Ddu, spreads little of its grandeur to the passing traveller. One has to 'get in there, and get at 'em', as the saying goes. Perhaps the better view of this sombre, and rather forbidding territory from any roadway, is that from the 'Mynydd Llan' road, high above the Usk reservoir.

The Bannau Brycheiniog, Fan Foel, and the Bannau Sir Gaer display their flanks to the north and east, each laying guard to the waters of their respective Llynns. And the man that has not witnessed the rays of a rising sun glistening across the sinister water of Llynn y Fan Fach, a little after the dawn, has skipped a page from the fascinating and mythological Welsh history. Not merely forbidding, the entire scene holds a spellbinding wonder.

Whereas our jaunts into the wilderness are usually well planned, the first 'boot and rucksack' sortie into this land of legend was a pure rush affair.

It was mid October and the season had been a busy one. The last of the 'booked in' guests had left, and a two day break at least we felt warranted. It was a case of, shut the door and run, or you never had a day off. In consequence, it poured down; all day long, all night long and we kicked our heels awaiting a break in the deluge.

All we could think of, I threw into the back of our dilapidated old van; a little 'banger' I would never have dreamed of using in the most frugal days of my market trading. But for all its coughing and spluttering, it let me down completely only once.

By the following afternoon the top of Pen-y-Fan was clear, and that's all we wanted; cloud level at 3,000 feet is good enough, and off we went, to arrive later in the pitch dark, way beyond the end of a made up road, and somewhere alongside a fast flowing stream that would have to wait the morrow before we had chance to pin point it on the map.

This then would be our 'pitch' for the next two nights, and the match box van our home; amongst the chaos in the back, sleeping bags were somehow laid out, and, as the night was comparatively young, we decided a couple of hours in the local would not go amiss.

The 'local' of course, was three times as far as you had imagined whilst driving to where we had holed-up. But the walk would do us good, and we trundled off into the black night; and in these areas wondering if they spoke English.

Yes, they did, and after a few badly accentuated "bora da's" and "diolch y fawr's" it was accepted that we had originated from the other side of the mountains, and the language switched to English; thank goodness!

For the entire evening there were only eight of us in the pub, all told. And after the first two pints we were going to hear all the well polished tales of intrigue and hilarity, performed hitherto by all the local characters. That was after they had learned everything of immediate consequence concerning ourselves.

There is always one eloquent individual who opts for the role of story teller. Here it was Jeff, 'the post'. And his repertoire was immutable, extremely funny, and so reminiscent of the stories told oft in our very own local.

Inevitably, the Welsh award their characters amusing pseudonyms, and here they had all the equivalents. 'Morgan, the milk', 'Jeff, the post', 'Jones, the knife' and 'Rees, the brush'; the latter two, butcher and painter respectively. In our own locality there were many; We had 'Dai, central 'eating', he the one who sported one tooth only, and that at the top centre of a cavernous opening twix nose and chin. 'Dai, pencil and paper', the traffic warden, everybody's enemy, and 'Davies, the tap' who worked for the Water Board. Davies's were many in our village, and apart from 'the tap', we had 'Davies, the post' and 'Davies, the crossing', she who worked the crossing gates in the days when a railway traversed the shire.

Perhaps the most baffling of these sobriquets however, was 'Dai, top shelf'. It appeared that David, Dai to any Welshman, was a self employed labourer who like his 'tipple' in any form, but preferably from the whisky bottle. He was perpetually hard up until some kind customer elected to pay his bill, and then Dai went berserk. Into the nearest pub in town he would catapult bellowing "top shelf today landlord"..... It may be pointed out that in those less affluent days a whisky was reserved for the wealthy..... it was double the price of a beer, and four times that of cider, and of course stood apart on the top shelf, a little out of reach.

Thus we wobbled back along the narrowing lane, convinced the road had jack-knifed, but eventually finding the van; _ after we had walked into it, that was. Then the rot set in. It was worse than any 'one man' tent I have ever had the experience of struggling into. We opened the rear doors from the outside, and the sleeping bags blew out. In the dark, I found the camping gas stove, but the canister had run out, and the refill was somewhere under the front seat, but that wouldn't lift because we had jammed a rucksack underneath, having no other room.

We would manage without supper it was decided, and it was then I knocked over a can of cold water, all over my sleeping bag. With that sorted out we eventually struggled in through the back doors and eased a couple of cramp riddled bodies between the feathers, then I leaned on an elbow to pull the doors to and lock up for the night; but the handle was missing. So I struggled out again, out again and into the rain which had just started, first to stub my bare toes on a protruding boulder, then trap my shirt pulling a stubborn side door to, and finally falling headlong over Dorothea who by that time considered herself a suitable candidate for the T.V. series, 'Some Mothers do 'ave 'em'. Yet all was eventual bliss as I lay relaxed some minutes later. From the gentle sounds of easy breathing at my side, it appeared my loved one was on the point of deep sleep. I relaxed further..... then I could have cried..... the twitch of that ultra sensitive muscle ..... an awful realisation ..... I hadn't had a pee!

Before the early hours had slowly died there was a feeling that I was distancing myself from past visions of an endearing husband, yet by daybreak all was forgiven. There was a sunrise that spelled joy to the walker. Water in the fast flowing stream that refreshed and rejuvenated. A glorious manifestation of all that was good in the great outdoors. If we lacked the camp fire of old, then the smell of the bracken, the low mist over the water, the bleat of a mountain sheep, and the taste of bacon fried in the open. They were the compensations.

And now to the Fans. It was the first of many incursions; often from the same site. And if you are the soul that revels in a marked absence of humanity, then this is the terrain to enchant.

From the brooding silence of Llynn y Fan Fach, over the snub nosed peaks of Bannau Sir Gaer and Fan Foel, to the Bannau Brycheiniog where at 2,630 feet you gaze down into the placid waters of Llynn y Fan Fawr. Untouched by man. A lake roadless, and free from the hand of the speculator. A watershed that spawns the source of the Usk, to wind its course to Newport; and yards away a stream, to become the Tawe, and plunge down to Swansea town.

To the east and unbroken vista of mountain and vale. The Brecon Beacons, and a distant Waen Fach. Whilst to the north the rolling line of the central Cambrians. These are gifts only to the man who uses his feet. In this terrain there is no way other to get there.

After walking the mountains of North Wales as a youngster, and those of the south in recent times, a natural progression would be to 'do the middle bit', and this is what we set about. This time with a more adequate form of overnight accommodation; a saloon car with the luxury of reclining seats. Means of cooking however, would remain the same, a camping gas stove, and under a roof of hopefully blue sky.

To the central Cambrians, where man made lakes abound, all tastefully engineered and with the minimum of spoilation. In fact it could be said the lakes of Elan Valley, Llynn Brianna and Clywedog are an endearing attribute to central Wales. That was our own consideration however, and for two years this wild country became our second home.

Sharing our enthusiasm for the wild uplands between Tregaron and Llanwrtyd, and twix Devils bridge and Rhayader were the million sheep that roam the wilds. As fellow 'naturists' they took no offence whatsoever when two fully mature pensioners rolled out of their car stark naked at seven in the morning. The only other living thing that did take some form of objection, were the million and one midges that seemed hellbent on destruction. At times they rivalled even the powers of their first cousins on the banks of several Scottish lochs I could name. Keep away from the water you were advised; the trouble was that this particular crowd appeared to have heard this advice also, and followed us just about everywhere we moved.

With the gift of retirement, being that of time, if not of hard cash, there was the means to stop, and to look; to plan, and to enjoy.

To that end we were now adroit. When the weathermen forecast a brief spell of suitable weather, we were off. If there was tankful of petrol we could aim afar. If not, there were several canal walks from Brecon, or the nearby scrambles around the Ystradfellte Waterfalls.

Aiming afar could mean the attraction of the Pembroke Coast Path, now designated a National Park. It was another in the growing sequence of long distance footpaths mushrooming across the country. The inception of the Pennine Way, the undertaking dreamed of by Ward Ogden and his fellow pioneers had heralded the onslaught of many of these projects, all to be acclaimed.

The walking of the Pennine Way, some three hundred miles of it, and in its entirety I doubt will ever come my way. Nevertheless, I have been privileged to tramp many an assorted section of that backbone of England, from Derbyshire to North Yorkshire, and for the future, who knows?

As to the present, it was the coast of Cardigan and Pembroke that called. In a series of four visits, and a succession of probably twelve days we walked what would most likely be deemed, the best part of the coastal path. Perhaps our favourite niche, a rather wild, and certainly the toughest section of the path, was the little bay of Ceibwr near Molygrove. A favourite haunt of the late writer and broadcaster Wynford Vaughan Thomas; a secure bay of rocks and pools for the seals and their pups, where the waves crash eternally into the hollowed cliffs and echo a sombre resonance. Yet perhaps not the scene, for the camp of a landsman, such as I.

In essence, that is what I am. And exhilarating as it was; the wind and the spray; the eternal sea and the rocks below me, the never ending sequence of climbing and dropping. Then an onshore wind that threatened to whisk me into the sea at any moment, and pounding waves that made to destroy the very path I walked. With respect, it was not for me, emphatically a landlubber.

Not inclined to brood over matters too long, I did give to wondering if my diminishing enthusiasm for rushing up mountainsides was anything to do with my age. It had been noticeable how much heavier the rucksack and boots were becoming. That fact, and possibly a couple of painful slips around the waterfalls of Scwd yr Eira and a ducking in the River Hepste had set us thinking of walks more on the plane of horizontality.

Thus there became and about turn in erstwhile dogma of yesteryear. By contrast we opted for walking the canal towpaths.

An exercise in matter over mind to reverse the axiom. Gone was the masochistic drive of youth that once sent us rushing up Snowdon in the depths of winter, or riding a bike across the moors of North Yorkshire at two in the morning.....

No, the placitude of calmer lands, and the gentle undulations of the low land became the attraction. And the towpaths of such a fine network of canals that exist could fit the bill.

Not only walking the canals, the exploration in itself is a stimulant. It became a fascination and we are still doing it today.

Be it the Corinth, the Kiel, the Manchester, or merely the more insignificant line of water that connects Brecon with Pontypool, they all hold a fascinating history.

On our own doorstep then the Brecon and Monmouthshire was an obvious starter, and again the car, or bicycle, a near necessity for the project in hand.

For thirty three miles this canal twines its mesmeric route through the Usk Valley, at times almost doubling back to meet itself; it is as if it never really wished to reach the sea at all. Not that it does now. Shortsighted planners of the 'silly' sixties saw to that, but the powers that be in today's less destructive age at least are becoming conscious of the heritage that their predecessors were hell bent on destroying. They are re-opening what has not been annihilated Of necessity the thirty three miles of this canal walk became sixty four, when we consider the car was left at a variety of convenient spots. and then a case of walking up to six miles or so, and retracing steps. This in effect did not cause any form of boredom; on the contrary it is surprising how different all appears when making an about turn.

A far wider contrast to the high peaks can hardly be imagined. The tranquil, almost unnoticeable flow of canal water, as opposed to the rushing torrent of a mountain stream in spate. The long boats inaudible clug as it drifts slowly by, and a hearty ''Good day'' from the boatman pierces an otherwise serene silence. Mallards nesting in the reeds, and a proud swan and its clutch of cygnets lazily drifting unheard. An overhang of willow steadily dusting the water's surface, and a sun that casts myriad shafts of colour through an endless curtain of virgin spinney.

Not always is that so; canals take in industrial black sports. That after all is what they were built for, commercialisation. But they are few now, and at least we now can take interest, from a heritage past.

In the fullness of time, we trod the last mile of the Brecon Canal, and as seemed our fate, within a short time were on the move to different pastures once again. Sixteen years had been our extended sojourn in Mid Wales, and throughout our stay we became more and more irrevocably captured by both the people and the land. But fate had turned the screw; It was our destiny to keep moving; once more a pantechnicon rumbled down the road. It was time to move again.

CHAPTER 17

UBIQUITOUS BOOTS

From the garden of 'The Coach and Horses', its willows lapping peacefully the Brecon Canal in Llangynidr, it is a far cry to the barren slopes of Cuesto Cielo, presiding with a majesty from the Sierra de Almijera, across the town of Nerja and along the southern coast of sub-tropical Spain.
We had arrived by motor caravan, and I sat on the patio, gazing across the brilliant blue Mediterranean. The local population were putting on their best, the children the costumes of tradition, for now they were about to let in the new year of 1990. Not only a far cry from Brecon, but from Morecambe where we had now chosen to live in Britain, and from the little house in Foundry Vale, Waterfoot where it all started. In one hand I held the deeds for the property we now rested in, whilst in the other I held a map.
I am never without a map. But this one had no right to be here. Along with an 'Ordnance' of the Lake District, this similar one of North Wales had found its way here among a multitude of continental road maps.
It could have secreted its way here by a twist of the subconscious when we were packing, because I am an inveterate map reader. From comments overheard I spend more time perusing the folds of these constant companions when we have returned from a venture, than ever I did before we set out. In all probability to discover what we had missed! If nothing else, it deepens the desire to return to a place of note, and on the second visit to pay substantially more attention.
Another great feature of this hobby, at least in my case, is the stirring of immeasurable nostalgia. At that I am incorrigible. Within seconds I float away into oblivion and recall the joys and the agonies of some foolish escapade in the dim and distant past.
So it was today with that sheet of Snowdonia. It jolted the memory of many cycle rides to a variety of Youth Hostels, of hikes from Snowdon Ranger Hostel, and the many times I drove commercial vehicles along that captivating coast, and through the evocative passes.
What did stand out most vividly however, was the ill-fated and dismal weekend I took my eldest son Douglas, at the age of twelve to view some 'real' walking country. At that time he was schooling in the tranquil surrounds of Henley-on-Thames, skirting the low lying pastures of the Chiltern Hills. A

devout 'southerner' he now was, having been taken there at the tender age of four. I so considered it time to introduce him to the granite, and the rugged contours of the North West.

We had rushed north in the estate car; just the two of us, and the sun had shone when we left, only to disappear in a mocking bank of grey cumulus as we approached the Midlands.

Arriving alongside Glyder-Fawr, we pulled in by the Afon Nant Peris some halfway down the Pass of Llanberis. The spot would suit for an overnight stop, and the clouds were high enough for a short reconnoitre, so off we went. There was just time to take in the lower slopes of Crib Goch before dark, and at the same time view our route up to Snowdon on the morrow.

It would not be an easy one. There were none as such on this flank, and was it nor on this very climb that our old friend, Eva Benson had fallen to her death. It all made me doubly cautious, and I knew well how important a fact was clear weather. I prayed for it, and we crawled our way into sleeping bags.

Intent on firing the imagination of the lad for the morrow, I related tales of yesteryear; scrambling the forbidding crags of the Glyders behind us, scaling the rock of the 'Devil's Kitchen' and viewing future Himalayan climbers practising their skills round the Idwal Slabs; Of the sombre magnificence of Llynn Idwal, and the exhilarations of a climb to the summit of an impressive 'Trefan'.

It appeared I was fighting a losing battle. As we dozed the rain started. It increased to a crescendo within an hour and battered on the car roof endlessly, ill determined we have little or no sleep whatsoever. By dawn, it had eased, and by the time we crawled out there was but a persistent drizzle. Alas the stream was in full spate, and I looked round; it was a sad sight, visibility was about thirty yards and the cloud blanketed us in an icy grip. A roaring torrent that was yesterday but a babbling brook took every exception when we attempted to either wash, or take water for drinking. We shivered and took in a scene of desolation and demoralisation..... What had I brought the lad up to see?

Knowing full well all the hidden dangers; setting one foot only on these evil slopes would be foolhardiness in the first degree. There was nothing else to it, all thought of any climb in these mountains today was abandoned, and we drove into Llanberis a miserable pair.

In a vain attempt to give the boy at least the possibility of a view of some description from the heights of Snowdonia, we took the mountain railway, much as it went 'against the grain'. That too was a disaster; for every yard of the journey the train enveloped itself in the pestilent fog, and it chugged it weary way to the summit and we saw nothing. So we returned to the car crestfallen, spent a couple of hours in the local cinema, and then dashed back pell mell to Henley-on-Thames; where of course, the sun had been shining all day!

The map slipped to the ground, I sipped at the second glass of Sangria and picked up that tattered, three shilling cloth sheet of the Lake District. It told me so much. Not merely of the days long ago, but of the immediate past. The two last years culminating in where I now sat gazing across a white walled Andalucian landscape. Almost all was delineated in these folds.

From the West Pennines of Lancashire to the mellow pastures of Wiltshire and Berkshire. Thence to the glorious hills of Mid Wales; and now a return to our native county. The very fringe that is, where shoulders rubbed with the charms of Cumbria. Could there exist a more fitting close to the life of the wanderlust? A house but a stone's throw from every conceivable delight to the walker. A centre I had dreamed to live in, over many a decade. All that now, and in addition a second home planted on the very edge of superb mountain slopes in far away Spain.

Putting the plan into operation, and two years later closing the little chapter had been a mammoth task. From selling one house, to storing furniture; to buying a motor home and subsequently two more houses, two thousand miles apart, was not the easiest of labours. Yet there were a host of compensations, some may even say we enjoyed an eighteen month holiday!

With a motor home, and awaiting the pleasures of house agents and solicitors, the scope for those of an outdoor motivation is tremendous, and we ourselves took every advantage of such a situation.

Given this luxury of total independence, the unexplored corners of Cumbria claimed first attention. To a little niche on the eastern fringe where my brother had quietly slipped on retirement. With his wife Marion, the Marion Cain of our cycling days, they had settled in the hamlet of Mosedale, a little out of range, from the massive onslaught of motorists that descend on the market town of Keswick.

Not only the inability to charge up the steepest slopes of a mountain, but the preference to seclusion, awarded us the delight of taking in both Skiddaw and Blencathra (Saddleback), from the little trodden north eastern flank. Admittedly less spectacular an approach, but on reaching the summit the equally rewarding panorama of Derwent Water and the Fells of Borrowdale, with mountains too numerous to name. These northern approaches are an exercise in solitude, and a blessed relief after you stand by the cairn with a multitude of backpackers and exhausted day trippers, and stare down at the town of Keswick below, and the track to it virtually pounded into a roadway, and fast eroding half the mountainside.

These more strenuous day long hikes were augmented by shorter, less ambitious walks in the glades and limestone outcrops of Arnside, Silverdale and Warton; that pocket sized gem of tranquillity given to the bird life of Morecambe Bay. Having cycled but never roamed the many pathways that abound hereabouts, it came our luck to find a site that could never have been excelled. With the motorhome firmly planted, there were little of the pathways left untrodden by the time our house keys came to hand.

When they did, the circle had been completed. We were back on native soil; the soil of the red rose. In the very county town of Lancaster no less. Here there was a canal too. One with the rural solitude, and the untroubled calm of the Brecon and Monmouth. Not the likes of the rat infested, bedstead and bike frame strewn water of the Leeds and Liverpool I left behind in Burnley forty years past. Instead, a canal of today, revived for the pursuits of pleasure, let it be for the boatman, the walker, the historian, or just the plain browser..... In the twilight of our walking days we now had that total gratification, and flowing through the centre of our very own city; the Lancaster canal.

Then what better than a repeat of our previous pattern. And where better to start than the wharf at Tewitfield. This is at present, the northernmost point of navigation in a waterway that originally saw canal boats plying the fifty seven miles from Preston to Kendal. Here the canal was severed, once more by shortsighted planning which thrust the M6 motorway northwards with reckless disregard to needs in the future.

Here at Tewitfield, there were eight locks, now a succession of weirs. They are the first you find, in a clever feat of engineering over the 41 miles from Preston, and hold a now amusing story; one which depicts the life and times of transport in the throes of a staggering change in the early days of the nineteenth century. It was the onslaught of the railways that saw the canal owners in a state of dismay. Here the 'Fly' or the 'Packet Boat' cruised supreme between Preston, Lancaster and Kendal. It had challenged and beaten the service of the stage coach, but now came the railway train; the one thing that was to change the entire concept of travel the world over, and the owners of this particular canal and its speedy service, were not to be beaten easily.

As the rails were spiked and clamped to sleepers that would take the dreaded steam train across the fells to Scotland, canalmen trimmed their boats, exchanged their horses for stronger and faster, and conceived more and more a plan to oust the rail threat.

Finally, before accepting the ultimate defeat the journey over this all but sixty mile of waterway was accomplished at the phenomenal average speed of eight miles an hour; that is double the speed of that recommended today! It entailed a change of horse every four miles, whilst at the Tewitfield locks passengers disembarked from their first 'packet boat', grabbed their luggage, and were urged to herculean efforts in running up the quarter mile pathway to the second 'fly' which awaited them at the head of the eight locks.

Reading these exploits does bring a posthumous streak of sympathy to mind for the poor horses involved, at times, whilst hauling these fully laden longboats they would be cantering at a speed in excess of ten miles an hour.

There will be many stories, and many miles to tread ere the last yard of towpaths on this canal we wander; Yet a narrative must find an ending somewhere.

I refolded the map. To the west the sun was kissing the horizon, dusting the shores of far away Morocco, and finally dipping beyond. That very same sun, the ball of fire that heaps its flame of orange across the Bay of Morecambe..... I mused..... It had been a poignant farewell, only yesterday? But no. It was all of six months past.

There were three of us. Three 'buddies' that held a close alliance. Ron Booth, Dorothea and myself. We shared an infinity; together we had long ago cycled one and every byway of the heart of Cumbria. The paths and the mountain tracks we three knew equally well. And that day an insatiable longing had drawn us to the remote and less frequented shores of Hawes Water. To the near vertical slopes of High Street, where golden eagles soar on wing, and wild deer roam the sparse grassland.

And for a final farewell, and a day to long remember what better than to stop, to stand, and to stare; from high on the fellside above Arnside. The panorama, viewed in pristine clarity is unchallengable. This evening gave us that perfection.

We sat enraptured; muted by the sheer magnificence.

A three dimensional fantasy. The setting sun to our left, momentarily brushing all an incandescent gold; the next a crimson red. Tinging the sea to a shimmering flame, whilst the entire spread of the lakeland mountains unfolded in silhouetted glory..... we lingered. The lights of Grange-over-Sands twinkled and slowly the evocative periphery grew in majesty; it appeared you could touch the peaks, from the western fringe of Harter Fell, across Scafell to the eastern bastion of High Stile. Even to the unmistakable contours of Ingleborough and away to the Yorkshire Dales.

It was a silent three; a reflective, possibly pensive trio that returned to the car. I stared at the car. At the wheels. Four this time and not two. Yet wheels I can fail to live without. Wheels that tomorrow would be bound for the dusty plains of Castilla-La-Mancha.

END